GLOBAL POWER FOR AMERICA

THERE ARE NUMEROUS wings assigned to Air Combat Command headquartered at Langley Air Force Base in Virginia, and they operate a variety of aircraft. From the HH-60W helicopter used for picking up military personnel isolated behind enemy lines, to the E-3G Sentry tasked with command and control, to the stealthy F-22 Raptor and F-35A fighter aircraft.

Air Combat Command is the lead for fighter, command and control, intelligence, surveillance and reconnaissance, personnel recovery, persistent attack and reconnaissance, electronic warfare, and cyber operations. It is responsible for providing combat air, space and cyber power, and the combat support that assures mission success to America's warfighting commands.

There are over 1,000 aircraft assigned to 27 wings based at non-expeditionary locations, and an additional eight wings at expeditionary locations for a total of 35 wings – nearly 1,400 units spread across 240 locations. The active duty, civilian and air reserve component have over 155,000 people assigned who are organised under five active duty numbered air forces and the Air Force Warfare Center.

All seven core operations and each aircraft type used to execute those operations are covered in extensive detail in this edition, specifically the A-10, E-3, F-15E, F-16, F-22, F-35, RQ-4, MQ-9, and RC-135.

Whatever your interest in aviation, this edition provides insight into a fascinating US Air Force organisation which provides around the clock global airpower for America, 365 days a year.

Mark Ayton
Editor

USAF/A1C Zeeshan Naeem

USAF/A1C Jonathan Koob

CONTENTS

USAF/A1C Lauren Sprunk

60 **The Gunslingers**

Moody Air Force Base, Georgia, has been home station to the A-10-equipped 23rd Fighter Group since 2007. The group will be the final A-10 operator in Air Combat Command.

70 **Snoopy Birds**

Offutt Air Force Base, near the city of Omaha in Nebraska, is home to the 55th Wing and its fleet of RC-135 reconnaissance aircraft.

86 **Jolly Green II**

Based at Moody Air Force Base, Georgia, the 41st Rescue Squadron has been in the combat search and rescue business with the HH-60 helicopter since 1989.

92 **Hill Lightnings**

The 388th Fighter Wing based at Hill Air Force Base, Utah, provides tactical strike and electronic attack capabilities with three squadrons of stealthy F-35A Lightnings.

96 **Shaping and Defining the Fight**

Based at Tinker Air Force Base, Oklahoma, the E-3G-equipped 552nd Air Control Wing operates to shape and define the air battle.

106 **Drone-based ISR**

A review of the MQ-9 Reaper and RQ-4 Global Hawk uncrewed aircraft used by the US Air Force for the intelligence, surveillance, and reconnaissance role.

ISBN: 978 1 83632 181 1
Editor: Mark Ayton
Senior editor, specials: Roger Mortimer
Email: roger.mortimer@keypublishing.com
Cover Design: Steve Donovan
Design: SJmagic DESIGN SERVICES, India
Advertising Sales Manager: Sam Clark
Email: sam.clark@keypublishing.com
Tel: 01780 755131
Advertising Production: Becky Antoniades
Email: Rebecca.antoniades@keypublishing.com

SUBSCRIPTION/MAIL ORDER
Key Publishing Ltd, PO Box 300, Stamford, Lincs. PE9 1NA
Tel: 01780 480404
Subscriptions email: subs@keypublishing.com
Mail Order email: orders@keypublishing.com
Website: www.keypublishing.com/shop

PUBLISHING
Group CEO: Adrian Cox
Publisher: Steve O'Hara

Published by
Key Publishing Ltd, PO Box 100, Stamford, Lincs. PE9 1XQ
Tel: 01780 755131
Website: www.keypublishing.com

PRINTING
Precision Colour Printing Ltd, Haldane, Halesfield 1, Telford, Shropshire TF7 4QQ

DISTRIBUTION
Seymour Distribution Ltd, 2 Poultry Avenue, London EC1A 9PU
Enquiries Line: 02074 294000

We are unable to guarantee the bona fides of any of our advertisers. Readers are strongly recommended to take their own precautions before parting with any information or item of value, including, but not limited to money, manuscripts, photographs, or personal information in response to any advertisements within this publication.

GLOBAL POWER FOR AMERICA

An overview and chronological history of Air Combat Command as compiled by the command's history office.

ALTHOUGH AIR COMBAT Command was activated on June 1, 1992, its predecessor, Tactical Air Command (TAC) traces its history back to March 1946.

During the 1950s, many of TAC's units were transferred to the Far East during the Korean Conflict and to Europe to bolster the North Atlantic Treaty Organisation, yet the command expanded. New units were formed, and new aircraft types were acquired to replace those transferred overseas.

In 1955 TAC developed a mobile strike capability for rapidly moving its units from the United States to any area of the world where a brush-fire war was threatened. Named the Composite Air Strike Force (CASF), it included fighters for delivering both conventional and nuclear weapons, transports for airlifting men and equipment, tankers for aerial refuelling, and reconnaissance planes for aerial photography. The CASF was designed to augment combat-ready units already assigned to US Air Forces in Europe (USAFE), the Pacific Air Force, and Alaskan Air Command.

Two years later, TAC was further strengthened when Strategic Air Command no longer needed fighter planes for bomber escort, and its fighter units were transferred to TAC.

The first actual employment of the CASF took place in July 1958 when the president of Lebanon called upon the United States to prevent the possible overthrow of his nation's government. Within three hours of receiving an alert, TAC had its planes on their way across the Atlantic to the Middle East. With TAC's nuclear forces in Turkey only 15 minutes away, the crisis in Lebanon gradually dissolved, and the CASF returned to the United States without having to engage in combat.

Six weeks later, TAC sent another CASF to the Far East because of a Chinese announcement that it intended to attack the island of Quemoy occupied by the Chinese Nationalists. In the face of the rapid reaction by US forces, the Communists did not carry out their threat.

In the autumn of 1961, TAC was called into action, this time to deploy men and aircraft to Europe because of the Berlin Crisis. Numerous US Air Force Reserve and Air National Guard (ANG) units were mobilised to increase TAC's combat strength, and in November TAC deployed more than 200 ANG aircraft and thousands of personnel under Operation Stair Step to France, Germany, and Spain to augment USAFE units already on duty in Europe. The crisis ended in the summer of 1962 and personnel returned to the United States.

In the mid-1960s, TAC underwent rapid growth. As a result of the increasing importance of tactical air power, plus the impact of the Vietnam Conflict, it practically doubled in size and strength. In the late 1960s, the Composite Air

Below: **RF-4C Phantom 67-0454/BA assigned to the 45th Tactical Reconnaissance Training Squadron, a component of the 67th Tactical Reconnaissance Wing once based at Bergstrom Air Force Base, Texas.** National Archive/USAF

Left: **An F-16C assigned to the 347th Composite Wing's 69th Fighter Squadron based at Moody Air Force Base, Georgia, uploads fuel from a KC-135, during a mission in 1997.** National Archive/USAF

Below: **F-15C 86-0152/EG assigned to the 58th Fighter Squadron on final approach to Eglin Air Force Base, Florida, home station of the 33rd Fighter Wing.** National Archive/USAF

Strike Force was replaced by the bare base concept which provided for air transportable packages of reusable shelters, munitions, fuel and other necessities. The bare base concept permitted a tactical air strike force to deploy into any suitable landing strip in the world and to operate independently without the usual resupply requirements.

Between 1950 and 1960, TAC's fighter force became totally supersonic with the assignment of the F-100 Super Sabre, F-101 Voodoo, F-104 Starfighter and F-105 Thunderchief. It was further strengthened between 1960 and 1970 by the delivery of the A-7D Corsair, F-4 Phantom, and F-111 Aardvark. At this same time, TAC provided aircraft, crews and support personnel for the constantly expanding Vietnam Conflict. TAC also developed Replacement Training Units in the United States to prepare air crews for combat in Southeast Asia. In addition to those requirements, seizure of the USS *Pueblo* by North Korean forces on January 23, 1968, required TAC to call up 18,000 Air Force Reserve and ANG personnel and equipment, and deploy

a large percentage of its strength to the Far East.

In the 1970s, TAC continued its modernisation programme with the addition of the F-15 Eagle, F-16 Fighting Falcon and A-10 Thunderbolt II. It was assigned operational control of all the US Air Force drones and remotely piloted vehicles in 1976, and a year later received its first E-3A Airborne Warning and Control System (AWACS) aircraft.

By the end of the decade, TAC had grown to 98,000 people and some 2,000 aircraft at 24 bases. Numerous Air Force Reserve and ANG units were assigned for immediate availability should the need arise. TAC also assumed responsibility for air defence of the United States against enemy manned aircraft when the Air Defense Command was dissolved late in 1979.

In World War Two, as the United States and its allies gained air superiority in the skies over Europe, the multifaceted role of tactical air power proved pivotal. The US War Department recognised tactical air as one of the three pillars of modern air power when it established the Tactical Air Command (TAC) on March 21, 1946, along with the Strategic Air Command (SAC) and Air Defense Command (ADC).

TAC complimented SAC's strategic mission to deliver an all-out nuclear punch with the tactical role of fighting limited wars with conventional arms. TAC Headquarters was initially activated at Tampa, Florida, on March 21, 1946, but was moved to Langley Field, Virginia, on May 21. This move was directed by Headquarters Army Air Forces to locate the headquarters closer to the Headquarters Army Ground Forces at Fort Monroe, Virginia, and the US Navy's Atlantic Fleet Headquarters in Norfolk, Virginia.

By the late 1940s, TAC became a key element in supporting America's national security and diplomatic objectives. With the sudden outbreak of the Korean War in June 1950, the command came of age when jet aircraft battled each other for the first time and US Air Force pilots, many of whom were TAC-trained, achieved overwhelming air superiority against their enemy counterparts. The command continued to grow after the war, and refined its mission as a force provider by ensuring it maintained a ready and mobile force.

TAC developed the Composite Air Strike Force concept in the 1950s, the precursor to the Air Expeditionary Force construct used during the 1990s.

The tensions of the Cold War heightened with the growing presence of US forces in Southeast Asia. During the early years of the Vietnam War, nearly 1,000 TAC fighter, airlift, reconnaissance,

Above: **Airmen assigned to the 43rd Electronic Combat Squadron pose for a group photo before boarding an EA-37B Compass Call II aircraft for its first official mission training sortie at Davis-Monthan Air Force Base, Arizona, on May 2, 2025.** USAF/Amn Samantha Melecio

Right: **Three F-4E Phantoms assigned to the 334th Tactical Fighter Squadron in formation over North Carolina during a mission from their home station, Seymour Johnson Air Force Base.** National Archive/ USAF

Below: **F-16A aircraft assigned to 474th Tactical Fighter Wing, once based at Nellis Air Force Base, Nevada, parked on a flight line during Exercise Solid Shield 1987 staged on the US east coast, the Caribbean, and Central America.** National Archive/ USAF

and special operations aircraft were deployed, along with thousands of pilots, maintainers, and support personnel. As the war continued, the command trained and equipped thousands of aircrews who eventually employed their skills in the skies of Southeast Asia. Throughout the remaining Cold War period, TAC focused its energy on maintaining the readiness of its forces, being prepared to gain and maintain air superiority, find, and destroy enemy forces and their support elements, provide for the air defence of the American homeland, and support its joint partners, the US Army and US Navy.

Following Vietnam, the command oversaw the development of new weapons systems such as the A-10, F-15, F-16, and F-117, aircraft types that would help to guarantee airpower's key role in meeting the nation's defence and national security objectives.

In August 1990, TAC forces were deployed overseas to help deter aggression as part of Operation Desert Shield and Desert Storm. In early 1991, about 470 aircraft and nearly 18,000 personnel from TAC formed the backbone and leadership of US Air Force elements which conducted one of the most successful air campaigns in history.

The collapse of the Soviet Union in late 1991 led senior US defence planners to conclude the Cold War structure of the military establishment which had continually grown over the previous 44 years was no longer needed in a unipolar world. While the likelihood of a large-scale nuclear war seemed more remote, US military forces would increasingly be called upon to participate in smaller-scale regional conflicts and humanitarian operations.

Consequently, the US Air Force began to reconsider the long-standing distinction between two major commands: SAC and TAC. The term 'strategic' had become almost totally linked to the notion of nuclear deterrence. The focus of 'tactical' operations, on the other hand, was on a co-operative mission, with the US Air Force working in tandem with ground and naval forces. The distinction, however, did not lend itself to a limited conflict. During the war in Southeast Asia, strategic B-52 bombers performed tactical missions (including close air support), while tactical fighter aircraft carried out strategic bombing deep in enemy territory. The conduct of Operation Desert Storm in early 1991 further blurred the distinction between the two terms. Consequently, as senior air force officials sought to re-examine roles and missions, the redundancy of this former division came under their scrutiny.

The birth of Air Combat Command (ACC) on June 1, 1992, took place amid momentous changes within the US Air Force and the Department of Defense. A brief ceremony at Langley Air Force Base, Virginia, marked the inactivation of TAC and the activation of ACC. As a new major command, it developed a new mission, not just as the successor of the former TAC and SAC. The command was responsible for providing combat-ready forces for deterrence and air combat operations. Upon activation, ACC assumed control of all fighter resources based in the continental United States, all bombers, reconnaissance platforms, battle management resources, and intercontinental ballistic missiles (ICBMs). Furthermore, ACC had some tankers and C-130s in its composite, reconnaissance, and certain other combat wings.

Right: **F-16A 80-0474/NA, the 474th Tactical Fighter Wing's flagship, rolls away from a tanker after aerial refuelling during Exercise Solid Shield 1987. The 474th was once based at Nellis Air Force Base, Nevada.** National Archive/USAF

Below: **F-4E Phantom74-1039/SJ assigned to the 4th Tactical Fighter Wing taxis out of a shelter at Ramstein Air Base, West Germany, during Exercise Crested Cap, the USAF component of the annual return of forces to Germany dubbed REFORGER.** National Archive/USAF

Since its activation in June 1992, ACC found itself in an almost constant state of flux. While eventually returning its ICBMs and bombers to Air Force Global Strike Command, as well as transferring its theatre airlifters and a part of its original flying training mission to other commands, ACC gained the combat rescue mission and oversees an extensive intelligence, surveillance, and reconnaissance (ISR) force. At the same time, sweeping changes in America's military policy, force structure reductions and a requirement for much greater flexibility were imposed on ACC.

ACC forces remain on call to perform a variety of missions, including support to international peacekeeping operations, to humanitarian needs at home and abroad, and protection of America's interests around the globe.

Throughout the 1990s and into the 2000s, ACC oversaw the development and implementation of the Air Expeditionary Forces (AEF) concept, which remains the primary method the US Air Force uses to deploy its forces across the globe.

The AEF played a major part in peacekeeping in the Balkans, in

counterterrorism efforts in Africa, and most especially in long-term operations in Southwest Asia since 2001. As the Combat Air Forces (CAF) lead, ACC continues to serve as the primary provider of air combat forces to America's warfighting commanders.

In August 2016, then Secretary of the Air Force, Deborah Lee James, approved a heritage action to merge the lineages of TAC and ACC. The decision to consolidate the two organisations came because of SAC's return to active service as the Air Force Global Strike Command in 2009. In addition, ACC has continued to use the TAC emblem as its own since 1992, thus combining the two commands and recognising that connection. The formal unification of TAC and ACC commands took effect on September 26, 2016, and allows the command to provide combat-ready airpower to America and its leaders.

The establishment of ACC in 1992 was entrusted to retired General John Loh, the final commander of TAC, who set his sights on defining an inclusive culture for the new command. Loh did not consider himself to be a pioneer, he was just fortunate and humbled enough to be named the first commander of ACC, and to set the stage and operating style of the command. According to Loh, this wasn't the old SAC or the old TAC, but a new command that

Above: **A-7D Corsair II 70-0955/EL assigned to the 76th Tactical Fighter Squadron once based at England Air Force Base, Louisiana, releasing two Mk82 high-drag bombs over a range at Fort Polk.** National Archive/USAF

required a new and different culture. He made communicating his intent for the new command a critical part of his leadership strategy. When he visited units, he ensured all airmen knew they were vitally important to the success of ACC's mission.

To improve readiness, the command instituted the Air Force Force Generation (AFFORGEN) model to replace the

Air Expeditionary Force deployment model. In short, AFFORGEN comprises four six-month phases: prepare, certify, available to commit, and reset, over a 24-month period. ACC is evolving its organisational structures, warfighting concept of operations, force presentation and generation, and how it prepares its airmen to ensure they are ready for strategic competition.

Right: **An F-4E Phantom assigned to the 35th Tactical Fighter Wing then based at George Air Force Base, California over the Saudi desert while on a training flight during Operation Desert Shield.** National Archive/ USAF

Milestones

July 1, 1993
ACC's ICBM mission, along with the 20th Air Force and FE Warren Air Force Base (AFB) transferred to Air Force Space Command.

July 27, 1993
The first female fighter pilot, 2nd Lieutenant Jeannie Flynn, began her F-15E course flight training at Luke AFB, Arizona.

August 11-13, 1993
Two B-1Bs from the 28th Bomb Wing at Ellsworth AFB, South Dakota, circumnavigated the globe for the first time and in a record-breaking 24.4 hours non-stop.

December 11, 1993
ACC officially accepted ACC-1 *Spirit of Missouri*, its first B-2 aircraft.

June 3, 1995
Two 7th Bomb Wing B-1Bs landed after completing a historic 36-hour, 13-minute, 20,100 mile, non-stop around-the-world flight.

August 25, 1995
A 2nd Bomb Wing B-52H Stratofortress and its five-member crew set an aviation world record from Edwards AFB, California, flying 5,400nm, unrefuelled, with a payload of 11,000lb – in 11 hours, 23 minutes with an average speed of 556mph.

August 31, 1995
ACC's first SR-71 Blackbird aircrew became fully mission qualified, with the second crew being qualified November 21, 1995.

June 11, 1996
The first production standard E-8 Joint Surveillance Target Attack Radar System aircraft was formally accepted by ACC and the 93rd Air Control Wing at Robins AFB, Georgia.

April 9, 1997
The first production standard F-22 Raptor was unveiled and named *Spirit of America*.

September 11, 2001
F-15 Eagles from the 1st Fighter Wing at Langley AFB, Virginia, were scrambled in response to the September 11 terrorist attacks.

December 30, 2002
ACC accepted its first F-22 Raptor.

January 22, 2006
The 27th Fighter Squadron from Langley AFB, Virginia, flew the first F-22 operational sorties in support of Operation Noble Eagle.

February 7, 2008
The first overseas operational deployment of the 12 F-22 Raptors from the 27th Fighter Squadron supporting the US Pacific Command's Theater Security Package in the Western Pacific.

March 6, 2013
ACC's first F-35s were delivered to Nellis and Edwards AFBs.

May 3, 2013
ACC declared Initial Operation Capability for the F-35A.

October 1, 2015
ACC officially transferred the B-1B Lancers of the 7th and 28th Bomb Wings and the Long-Range Strike-Bomber Program to Air Force Global Strike Command, placing all strategic command bomber assets under a single Major Command.

September 1, 2017
As the first operational F-35 unit, the 34th Fighter Squadron at Hill AFB, received its 26th and final Block 3F F-35A.

June 7, 2018
US Air Force officials announced the service's cyber responsibilities would realign to ACC from Air Force Space Command.

April 15, 2019
ACC F-35A Lightning II's from the 4th Fighter Squadron at Hill AFB deployed into combat for the first time.

April 30, 2019
Two US Air Force F-35A Lightning IIs conducted the type's first combat air strikes in support of Combined Joint Task Force – Operation Inherent Resolve.

October 11, 2019
ACC activates 16th Air Force at Joint Base San Antonio-Lackland, Texas, integrating 24th Air Force along with Air Force Cyber and 25th Air Force into a single headquarters to provide global intelligence, surveillance and reconnaissance, cyber, electronic warfare, and information operations.

Below: EC-130H Compass Call aircraft 73-1594/DM assigned to the 41st Electronic Combat Squadron taxies at Davis-Monthan Air Force Base, Arizona. Now in the twilight of its service life, the EC-130H can jam communications, navigation systems, early warning and acquisition radars. The type is being replaced by the EA-37B Compass Call II. USAF/A1C Jasmyne Bridgers-Matos

August 20, 2020
ACC activated 15th Air Force (AF), integrating wings and direct reporting units from the 12th AF and 9th AF to form the 15th AF, responsible for generating and presenting ACC's conventional forces.

October 29, 2020
The first iteration of Exercise Agile Flag ended. The experiment was a stepping stone to the ability to deploy into theatre as Lead Wings.

November 5, 2020
The 23rd Wing and 347th Rescue Group leadership received the Air Force's first two HH-60W Jolly Green II helicopters at Moody AFB, Georgia.

April 20, 2021
ACC received its first F-15EX Eagle II at Eglin AFB, Florida.

June 25, 2021
Recognising an operational need to dominate the electromagnetic spectrum, ACC temporarily activated the 350th Spectrum Warfare Wing (SWW) at Eglin AFB while the air force conducted an environmental review for the permanent location. The 350th SWW enables, equips, and optimises fielding capabilities to give the US and its allies a sustainable,

competitive advantage over adversaries in the electromagnetic spectrum.

January 5, 2022
General Mark Kelly, then commander of ACC, designated five units as Lead Wings as part of the combat air force's transition to the service's new force generation model. The following wings were notified to be ready to rapidly generate combat power as a deployed force: 4th Fighter Wing, Seymour Johnson AFB, North Carolina; 23rd Wing, Moody AFB, Georgia; 55th Wing, Offutt AFB, Nebraska; 355th Wing, Davis-Monthan AFB, Arizona; and 366th Fighter Wing, Mountain Home AFB, Idaho.

July 12, 2023
The E-8C Joint STARS-equipped 12th Airborne Command and Control Squadron (ACCS) flew its last operational flight at Robins AFB, Georgia. The 12th ACCS was the last JSTARS squadron to take flight as part of the 461st ACW.

August 30, 2023
The 85th Test and Evaluation Squadron had recently validated the F-15EX Eagle II's employment of the AGM-158 Joint Air-to-Surface Standoff Missile (JASSM) during the 53rd Wing's Weapons System Evaluation Program.

September 11, 2023
Then Secretary of the Air Force, Frank Kendall, announced the Air Task Force as the next step in the AFFORGEN model.

January 26, 2024
The US Air Force Warfare Center's first iteration of Bamboo Eagle began on January 26. The eight-day exercise took place in various locations across the United States and designated sea and airspace in the eastern Pacific, designed to provide advanced training in a disaggregated, multi-domain scenario to sustain and strengthen the ability of the joint and coalition force to prevail in conflict when necessary.

September 23, 2024
ACC activated three Air Task Forces as pathfinders to help the US Air Force understand the necessary support and training airmen will need to form Combat Wings as units of action to present to combatant commands.

October 7, 2024
To meet the challenges of Great Power Competition, General Ken Wilsbach, then commander of ACC, outlined a vision for the future by emphasising four key focus areas for the command: readiness, modernisation, agile combat

Below: **F-15A Eagles, 77-0129/HO and 77-0142/HO, assigned to the 8th Tactical Fighter Squadron, once based at Holloman Air Force Base, New Mexico, at Elmendorf Air Force Base, Alaska, during Exercise Cope North 84-3.** National Archive/USAF

employment (ACE), and taking care of airmen and families.

April 11, 2025
The US Air Force celebrated 50 years of Red Flag – an aerial combat training exercise co-ordinated at Nellis AFB and conducted over the Nevada Test and Training Range.

The exercise is a major element in advancing realistic, multi-domain training for US, joint and coalition forces.

May 12, 2025
The F-22 Raptor reached two decades of operational service at Langley Air Force Base on May 12, 2025.

May 14, 2025
The 43rd Electronic Combat Squadron flew the first mission training sortie with the EA-37B from Davis-Monthan AFB on May 2, 2025. The EA-37B wide-area airborne electromagnetic attack weapon system is replacing the legacy EC-130H.

July 8, 2025
US Air Force pilots flew two XQ-58A Valkyrie autonomous collaborative platforms (ACPs), alongside their F-15E Strike Eagle and F-16C Fighting Falcon aircraft in an air combat training scenario from Eglin AFB, Florida, demonstrating real-time integration between manned and semi-autonomous systems.

July 12, 2025
Two F-15EX Eagle II aircraft from the 85th Test and Evaluation Squadron based at Eglin AFB, arrived at Kadena Air Base, Japan, on the type's first overseas deployment.

August 5, 2025
Hosted by the US Air Force Warfare Center, Bamboo Eagle 25-3 was the final exercise in the Department of the Air Force's Department-Level Exercise series, incorporating multiple command exercises into one overall threat deterrence scenario, including Resolute Force Pacific, Resolute Space, Mobility Guardian, and Emerald Warrior.

Above: **An A-10A Thunderbolt II assigned to the 354th Tactical Fighter Wing once based at Myrtle Beach Air Force Base, South Carolina, undergoing maintenance during Exercise Quick Thrust 1983-1.** National Archive/ USAF

QUARTERBACK

Based at Langley Air Force Base, Virginia, the F-22 Raptor-equipped 1st Fighter Wing has been in the fighter business since 1918. This section provides insight into the Wing's mission, aircraft, and maintenance.

WATCHING AN F-22 pilot work through his pre-flight checks at Langley Air Force Base (AFB), you appreciate how the fifth-generation aircraft looks up close, and absorb the sound of the two Pratt & Whitney F119 turbofan engines when running. Valued at $143m, with the appearance of a fighting machine created for a far-fetched Hollywood movie, the F-22 looks every bit the super fighter that provides America with a capability advantage currently unmatched by any potential aggressor.

Often dubbed the silver bullet, the F-22 Raptors serving with four US Air Force fighter wings were all 'born and raised' in Cobb County, Georgia. More specifically at Air Force Plant No.6, the huge aircraft production facility at Marietta run by Lockheed Martin. Perhaps more famous for its C-130 Hercules assembly line, in constant production for 63 years, the last F-22 Raptor, serial number 10-4195, rolled out of the Marietta facility on December 13, 2011.

Many of the Block 30 and Block 35 F-22s built in the final production lot are assigned to the 1st and 192nd Fighter Wings based at Langley. The 192nd is an associate unit from Virginia's Air National Guard.

Fighting first

Langley-based F-22s flown by the 27th Fighter Squadron (FS) were the first to see combat in the autumn of 2014 at the beginning of Operation Inherent Resolve (OIR).

During the six-month deployment, the F-22s participated in the coalition air offensive against the so-called Islamic State (ISIS) in Iraq and Syria, undertaking a mix of deliberate pre-planned strikes and dynamic targeting strikes using 1,000lb GBU-32 JDAMs (Joint Direct

Attack Munitions) and 250lb GBU-39 small diameter bombs.

F-22s are frequently involved in large strike packages, helping other aircraft work through the threats, as was the case in Operation Midnight Hammer when F-22s assigned to the Langley-based 94th FS performed the offensive counter air role for B-2 Spirit bombers en route to Iran's nuclear facilities at Natanz and Fordo.

Combat operations over Syria during OIR presented all coalition pilots with a unique situation. They were involved in a Civil War against a portion of the counter regime forces, the Syrian Air Force remained active, the integrated air defence system was still functional, and Russian aircraft were also flying combat operations. That meant a lot of different assets were flying around which required a lot of co-ordination between the entities present there.

F-22s were utilised to keep an eye on all the different players involved in an environment probably unlike anything the US had undertaken before. The battlespace presented a high degree of complexity, and some uncertainty to all pilots. Those flying F-22s were well prepared, the training protocols followed by all F-22 squadrons is to the most challenging set of circumstances in a high-end fight. The F-22 community never backs off from such training scenarios, providing pilots with experience and a surplus of capacity such that when in a complex environment, but not the high-end threat trained against, they can work through the challenges and uncertainty, and still perform well.

Under the F-22's increment 3.2B modernisation effort, the aircraft received the capability to employ AIM-9X Sidewinder missiles and AIM-120D AMRAAM (advanced medium-range air-to-air missiles), an enhanced stores management system for the integration of new weapons and to improve weapon employment, improvements to the intra-flight datalink and electronic protection systems, and the aircraft's emitter geolocation capability, and gained a common weapon employment zone function to help the pilot employ air-to-air missiles.

The AIM-9X is fitted with a passive infrared target acquisition system, proportional navigational guidance, a closed-loop position servo fin actuator unit, and a target detector. Four forward-mounted fixed wings provide aerodynamic lift and stability, and four control fins mounted in line with the fixed wings manoeuvre the missile. A jet vane control provides enhanced manoeuvrability by deflecting rocket motor thrust to aid turning. The 9X missile has a different engagement zone to earlier variants, but its employment procedures are similar.

The AIM-120 AMRAAM is radar-guided with capability in both the beyond-visual-range and within-visual-range arenas. The missile uses a combination of inertial guidance, midcourse updates, and an on-board active radar to find the intended target and complete the intercept.

The AIM-120D is the newest variant which features improved high off boresight capability, internal GPS, enhanced two-way datalink, improved kinematics, and new software

Below: **An F-22 Raptor aircraft assigned to the 1st Fighter Wing takes off from Langley Air Force Base, Virginia.** USAF/ Nicholas De La Pena

Above: **Capt Nick Le Tourneau, pilot and commander of the F-22 Raptor Aerial Demonstration Team, flies an F-22 Raptor during the night show at EAA AirVenture, Oshkosh, Wisconsin, on July 26, 2025.** USAF/SSgt Lauren Cobin

improvements over the AIM-120C3 through C7 variants.

The AMRAAM programme develops iterative improvements completed under the System Improvement Program (SIP), each to enhance missile performance and to resolve previous deficiencies. AIM-120D3, the latest sub-variant, incorporates the form, fit, function hardware refresh to replace obsolete components, and uses SIP-3F operational flight program software.

Flying and fighting the Raptor

Discussing what the F-22 is like to operate and how it handles, former 1st Fighter Wing commander, Maj Gen Pete Fesler began by comparing what was required in the F-15C Eagle: "When I started the F-15 I had 15 minutes of programming, turning on systems and running built-in tests on each avionics system in the cockpit. I had to select each one and take particular steps to make sure the system was working. From engine start to when I taxied, all of that time involved selecting a system to programme. Even while taxiing, I would still be doing more of that which taxes your mind before you've even got going.

"In the F-22, I start it and the aircraft is by and large testing all of its systems by itself. I push one button to test the flight controls and let them go, I wait for everything to power up, I load data programmed onto a data transfer cartridge that runs everything so then I'm in the margins of, 'how would I prefer my displays to look for me today?' 'What do I want the displays to look like?' I might prefer one particular display to be shown in a certain manner and choose to place one display on the left and another on the right to suit my habit patterns for the way I prefer to process information.

"Most of what I do in that 15-minute window is waiting for the jet to time in and make some small adjustments to how I prefer to see things. The workload is much lower.

"We typically stop on the end of runway ramp to allow a crew to look over the aircraft one final time before we launch. That's not a necessity for the aeroplane and the crew does not have to pull pins from the jet before launch to arm. In many locations we roll straight out of the chocks to the runway on take-off.

"The amount of power in the F-22 is incredible, we do not do afterburner take-offs because there is no reason to, even with 8,000lb of external fuel carried in drop tanks, there is just no need to.

"It's very nimble on the controls. You barely touch the stick to make adjustments. Like most fighters, you do not have to hand fist it around; you just touch the stick and the aeroplane rolls using minor adjustments to change it."

Discussing the control of the Raptor, Fesler said: "What's unique about the F-22 is that anywhere in its performance envelope the pilot is not commanding a particular flight control surface to move but commanding a particular behaviour out of the aeroplane. Computers figure out what flight control surfaces to move, so moving the stick side-to-side does not automatically generate ailerons moving opposite each other, it might be rudders that move or a combination of 'stabs' and leading-edge flaps; it depends on what environment the aeroplane is in at the time.

"The F-15 was a smooth aeroplane and very nimble on the controls, but

Left: **The combined thrust with afterburner of two Pratt & Whitney F119-PW-100 turbofan engines amounts to 70,000lb.** USAF/SSgt Lauren Cobin

when I put 'g' on the F-15 it would shake, buffet and 'talk' to you. It told you where you were in the flight envelope based on what it sounded and felt like. The F-22 is also very smooth, and it talks to you a little bit, but not much. Think of the vibration felt in your car when you are sitting at idle compared to driving over rumble strips on the side of the highway – that's the sensory difference between the two aircraft."

Man compared to machine

Aircraft like the F-22 Raptor and F-35 Lightning II have what are termed as fusion engines; powerful computers that fuse all flight and sensor data together to provide the pilot with an overview of the battlespace throughout the mission. Discussing this capability on the F-22, Fesler said: "From an employment standpoint, much of my time in the F-15

Below: **An avionics technician assigned to the F-22 Raptor Aerial Demonstration Team, conducts a pre-flight inspection so the aircraft is mission ready.** USAF/SSgt Lauren Cobin

was spent trying to be the fusion engine, to take the data from the federated systems and build a three-dimensional picture in my mind and then communicate it. In the F-22, fusion is done for me and to a large degree the communication is done for me as I export the fused picture [via the intra flight datalink] out to other F-22s. That takes the workload away so I can focus on where I want to put my aeroplane to optimise the offensive capability or to have the greatest survivability.

"Do I have enough excess capacity to do that for everybody else in the battlespace? For example, where should I send the F-15Es, the F-16s, the F/A-18s? Because I do not have to work through the sensor feeds [to build a picture of the battlespace], I can go 'F-15Es it would be best if you go to here to target this group [of threats], this is the ID and this is how far they are from you'; 'F-16s this is what you have in front of you. Go get those threats and this is the best place for you.' It's quarterbacking from a fighter cockpit; in other words, airborne command and control from a fighter cockpit."

Reflection

Comparing his former mount, the F-15C Eagle, to the fifth-generation F-22

Raptor, Fesler noted how the new jet has changed tactics: "What is interesting is when I was a new wingman flying the F-15, my job was to stay visual with number one; he would get me to the merge and I would find my one target on the way in and shoot it. Today, because the processes involved with searching for and engaging a target is all automatic, I ask my F-22 wingmen to act as an airborne manager of the air battle space not just their cockpit or a two ship. That's asking a lot of our young pilots, but the aeroplane helps to do that.

"Automation of the F-22's sensors makes a missile shot a lot easier. While I'm in the process of prosecuting an attack, my aeroplane is continuing to look for and track other threats. The F-15 requires a lot more management of its sensors and once I started to employ a missile, my situational awareness would shrink down. In the F-22, my situational awareness is maintained which makes this part of the mission a lot easier. In addition, the ability to remain supersonic for extended periods of time without the use of afterburner is a tremendous

capability and certainly changes the employment of weapons as well."

Portable Magnetic Aircraft Covers

While he was working as a crew chief for the 1st Aircraft Maintenance Squadron, TSgt Daniel Caban devised a new concept for F-22 Raptor intake covers to improve existing maintenance practices.

Caban's creation was named the Portable Magnetic Aircraft Cover (PMAC) made of Polymagnets and Nomex IIIA fibres, covers that can be folded and packed into a small compartment on the aircraft. The PMAC design eliminated the need for the Dash 21 covers, which require separate shipping to the aircraft's predisposed location due to their size.

Caban chose Nomex IIIA because of its electrostatic and hydrophobic properties, which allow the material to breathe while withstanding water. Specialised magnets adhere to rigid structures without interrupting sensitive electronic components nearby and mitigate damage due to wear on the jet's low-observable coating.

Dash 21 sets are made up of foam pads, which occupy 13.1ft^3 and cost $11,000 each. Each jet requires three Dash 21 sets to ensure the intakes and sensitive openings are protected at each location the pilot lands during missions. Caban's new design was estimated to have a production value that amounts to less than half of Dash 21 gear production cost, and measures at 567in^3.

The compact size proved advantageous and cost effective in terms of shipping since the set travels with the jet, allowing aircraft maintainers at various locations to apply the covers anytime they are needed.

Maj Brian Pascuzzi, then 1st Fighter Wing chief of wing plans and founder of the innovation cell, said: "When we looked at the deployment costs and the readiness enhancement that's possible with this idea, that's really where you get the 'bang for your buck' as far as PMAC goes."

Caban's was one of the first ideas presented during a pitch session where airmen exhibited their ideas to the innovation board, which included the

Below: **The first two F-22 Raptors assigned to the incoming Formal Training Unit (FTU) aircraft fleet, taxi at Langley Air Force Base, Virginia, on March 29, 2023. The FTU's move from Tyndall Air Force Base, Florida, involved the bed down of 30 additional F-22 Raptors at Langley and the establishment of the 71st Fighter Squadron as the FTU.** USAF/A1C Mikaela Smith

wing commander, the maintenance group commander, and other senior leaders.

Following the initial presentation, Pascuzzi and other innovation cell members worked with Caban to create a pathway that led him to the first phase of production, where he partnered with a local Hampton Roads business to produce a PMAC prototype made at no cost to the unit.

Caban's PMAC was a finalist in the US Air Force's 2020 Spark Tank competition, which prompted AFWERX, the US Air Force's innovation and technology group based in Austin, Texas, to award production contracts to Kennon Aircraft Covers based in Sheridan, Wyoming.

Fighter generation squadrons

The 1st Fighter Wing activated the 27th and 94th Fighter Generation Squadrons (FGS) at Langley on June 16, 2022. As part of the Combat Oriented Maintenance Organisation initiative, the activation of the FGS units embodies the US Air Force's commitment to evolution

Capt Nick Le Tourneau, F-22 Raptor Aerial Demonstration Team commander, performs a high-performance aerial manoeuvre during the Cocoa Beach Air Show in Florida, on July 12, 2025. USAF/SSgt Lauren Cobin

Above: **Lt Col Andrew Gray, then 71st Fighter Squadron commander, taxies an F-22 Raptor at Langley Air Force Base, Virginia, on March 29, 2023. As commander of the 71st FS, Gray led the way by taxiing one of the first F-22 Raptors onto the flight line.** USAF/A1C Mikaela Smith

Left: **An F-22 Raptor uploads fuel from a KC-10A Extender aircraft in the US Central Command area of responsibility. The F-22 assigned to the 27th Fighter Squadron was deployed from Langley Air Force Base, Virginia.** USAF/SSgt Michael Keller

and striving to continue synchronisation between maintenance and operations.

Col Neal Van Houten, 1st Maintenance Group commander, said: "The FGS units represent the first time in 1st Fight Wing history that squadron-level maintenance will control resources and priorities within its own unit. The activation marks the transition of approximately 700 maintenance airmen being redistributed under the newly enacted units. This structure provides many benefits to our airmen. It aligns them with a commander who can become fully immersed in tactical level execution while strategically advocating for their needs."

Innovation

In line with the vision of then US Air Force Chief of Staff, Gen Charles Brown Jr, the 1st Fighter Wing (FW) developed a team to transform its airmen's innovative ideas into reality.

TSgt Joseph Samples, non-commissioned officer in charge of the 1st FW's innovation cell, said: "Our primary function is to aid individuals in developing effective solutions and the process of making their ideas into tangible pieces.

"Major Mendel, an Air Combat Command Weapons and Tactics pilot, came to the innovation cell and addressed an issue with a sniper case he and the other pilots had to regularly carry. Mendel said 'My fingers hurt whenever I carry it. I wouldn't consider it

Mitchell Trophy Air Race

After a near 88-year hiatus, the Mitchell Trophy Air Race returned to Langley on March 6, 2025, with modernised rules and eligibility requirements.

The exclusive race involved a 446nm flight from Langley to Selfridge Air National Guard Base (ANGB), Michigan, and then back after completing various tasks performed by the pilots at Selfridge in accordance with the agile combat employment concept of operations. Participating pilots were required to land, park, refuel and launch their own jet. In addition, the competitors were required to run 1.6 miles from their parking spot to the Selfridge Museum to sign a historical logbook. All three 1st FW squadrons competed in the race: the 27th, 71st and 94th Fighter Squadrons.

First established in 1922, the Mitchell Trophy Air Race honoured 1st Lt John Lendrum Mitchell Jr, a pilot from the 1st Pursuit Group who died in a flying accident in France during World War One.

something in need of innovation, it's just a problem.'"

Together, they began to think about how to make the handle more comfortable to carry. They created a 3D printed model and soon had a fully developed handle that was no longer painful to hold.

"The work we are doing is important because it's teaching people very important lessons," said Samples. "It gives them that little bit of hope by knowing they have a way to approach challenges and not be stuck dealing with a problem. We are here to create lasting change, big or small, for the Air Force."

Pascuzzi said: "Airmen directly tasked with getting the job done, often have incredible insights on how to do things faster, better and cheaper. Any one of us can be innovative and make a huge difference if we are given the tools and the support to bring our ideas to fruition."

Pascuzzi and Samples agreed that the PMAC had been one of the most successful designs created within the innovation cell. Caban's concept continues to spread, and the F-35 community has started developing a similar idea based on his model.

Concluding, Samples said: "Airmen are dealing with everyday problems and don't know where to go. We need airmen to know that the innovation cell is here. If there is a problem, there is a solution – it's not something they just have to deal with."

Tyndall to Langley

The first two F-22 Raptors, part of the incoming Formal Training Unit (FTU) aircraft fleet, landed at Langley on March 29, 2023. These were the first of

Above: **An F-22 Raptor assigned to the 1st Fighter Wing based at Langley Air Force Base, Virginia, flies off the wing of a KC-46A Pegasus operated by aircrew assigned to the 22nd Air Refueling Wing, McConnell Air Force Base, Kansas, during Exercise Bamboo Eagle 25-3 on August 6, 2025, off the coast of California.** USAF/SSgt Tryphena Mayhugh

Right: **Capt Nick Le Tourneau, F-22 Raptor Aerial Demonstration Team commander, performs a high-performance manoeuvre during the Milwaukee Air & Water Show in Wisconsin, July 19, 2025.** USAF/SSgt Lauren Cobin

30 additional F-22 Raptors previously operated by the 43rd FS based at Tyndall AFB, Florida, the F-22 FTU since 2002. During its 20 years at Tyndall, the 43rd FS trained 830 F-22 pilots, eight of whom were in class 23-ABR, the last for the 43rd FS.

Above:
Condensation plumes over the wings of an F-22 during a flight demonstration.
USAF/SSgt Lauren Cobin

His brother, Col Billy Mitchell, introduced the trophy to commemorate his brother's legacy and promote airpower. The race was historically hosted at Selfridge Field, now Selfridge ANGB, home of the 127th Wing, until its suspension after the 1936 competition. After brief appearances in the 1960 and 1962 William Tell competitions, the trophy was eventually forgotten until rediscovered in 1998 at Seymour-Johnson AFB, North Carolina.

Col Brandon Tellez, 1st FW commander said: "The race was strategically important in preparing airmen for modern combat operations. The 1st Fighter Wing will face adversaries that are resourceful and determined to disrupt our tactics, techniques, and procedures in all phases of combat. Our airmen must be able to execute effective combat operations in dynamic environments that lack information and time."

The new Mitchell Trophy Air Race is specifically designed to enhance combat effectiveness and resilience by boosting performance through competition and camaraderie, enhancing agile combat employment resilience, testing physical, mental, and logistical limitations, and for identifying the top talent in the wing.

Returning to Selfridge ANGB to resume the race was symbolic as it marked the return of the 1st FW to the event's historical roots and paid tribute to the original home of the 1st Pursuit Group.

Lt Col 'Devil', commander of the 94th FS and winner of the air race, highlighted the support provided by their load crew, and the teamwork of the squadron. The team's success demonstrated the effectiveness of integrated operations between aircrews and maintainers under realistic, stressful conditions.

20 years of operational service

The F-22 Raptor achieved its 20th anniversary of operational service at Langley AFB on May 12, 2025 – the first combat-ready F-22 Raptor was delivered to Langley for the 1st FW on May 12, 2005.

The first aircraft, tail 4042, was flown from the Lockheed Martin facility in Marietta, Georgia, to Langley by Lt Col James Hecker, then commander of the 27th FS. Today Gen Hecker serves as commander, US Air Forces in Europe and Commander, US Air Forces Africa. Here's how he recounted the arrival: "Timing is everything. I wasn't supposed to be the first F-22 operational squadron commander. It was going to be Lt Col Scott Maw, but then the airplane delivery date slipped a little to the right, another squadron became available with the F-15 Eagle, so he took that command."

Hecker recalled the day he picked up the aircraft and acknowledged the importance of his team on the day: "It was obviously an honour for me, but it wouldn't have been possible if it wasn't for all the people in the squadron who prepared to make it happen. I remember going to Marietta, Georgia. We took an F-15 out there; a guy by the name of 'Corky' Corcoran was with me. We signed over what they call a DD250 [Department of Defense Material And Inspection Receiving Report], and it had a price tag on it. I've never written a cheque that expensive in my life."

Col Brandon Tellez, 1st Fighter Wing commander, said: "Twenty years later, it's still controlling the skies. The F-22 continues to dominate requirements in high-end

Above: **An F-22 Raptor prepares to refuel from a KC-135R Stratotanker over the Atlantic Ocean off the Virginia coast during a mission from Langley Air Force Base.** USAF/MSgt Keith Baxter

Left: **The F-22 Raptor's design features the distinctive chine and many angular components.** USANG/SrA Sarah Post

combat simulations and real-world operations. In that time the 1st FW has taken the Raptor to 20 different countries around the world. The F-22 Raptor continues to maintain its relevance against evolving threats. Our adversaries have continued to improve their capabilities and tactics, but so have we. The F-22 remains the most capable air superiority platform in the world and will continue to be vital for success for another 20 years."

The 1st Fighter Wing is responsible for the full F-22 training pipeline for all new Raptor pilots through the 71st FS and 1st Training Support Squadron, two combat-coded fighter squadrons, the 27th and 94th, with nearly half of the F-22 fleet assigned.

Summing up, Hecker said: "I think the big thing is that the world is catching up. It is a little bit more of an even fight than it was 20 years ago, so we have to make sure we're working harder and continue to be the best at the business of what we do."

FOURTH BUT FIRST

Based at Seymour Johnson Air Force Base, North Carolina, the F-15E equipped 4th Fighter Wing continues to provide unprecedented tactical strike capabilities to US combatant commanders.

WITH FOUR F-15E-EQUIPPED fighter squadrons assigned, the 4th Fighter Wing is the largest Strike Eagle wing in the US Air Force. Two of its component units, the 333rd and 334th Fighter Squadrons, are F-15E Flying Training Units, and the 335th and 336th Fighter Squadrons are combat-coded.

Each Flying Training Unit (FTU) runs courses to train F-15E pilots and weapon systems officers (WSOs), either those that are brand new to the aircraft or those transitioning back to Strike Eagle after a time away. The latter includes senior-ranked officers promoted to leadership positions within F-15E-equipped units.

After completing undergraduate pilot or combat systems officer training and a two-month introduction to fighter fundamentals course to learn the basics of flying fast jets, with Flying Training Wings commanded by Air Education and Training Command, brand new officers arriving at an FTU spend approximately ten months on the B-course learning to fly and operate the Strike Eagle.

Other than specific daily briefings, pilots and WSOs are paired together at the start of the course and work as a crew throughout. From the start, this approach builds the synergistic relationship required for the two-person F-15E crew under the adage 'one plus one equals something much greater than two'. The crew of two must each learn what the other one is attempting to do and build upon that without having to do the other person's job, something that's foundational to the mission.

Course outline

The first 40 days are spent in classrooms and operating device trainers under the instruction of former Strike Eagle instructors working for contractors who teach the basic aspects of the aircraft and provide insight as to what to expect when the crews first start to operate the jet. This includes sessions in an integrated avionics trainer (a mock cockpit) in which they work through basic missions, learning how to work the aircraft's avionics and systems.

This is followed by sessions in a 360° (but not full motion) simulator in which crews conduct basic missions before their first flight. Crew transition to the aircraft, typically around the midway point of the course, but before they go to the flight line, they use virtual reality (VR) technology to complete virtual walk arounds of a jet for familiarity, most notably on the day or evening before they are due to fly for the first time. The air force introduced VR systems in 2019.

Based on data analysis, the 4th Fighter Wing determined that the proximity of simulator sessions to flights gives better outcomes to training events, but equally showed no statistical significance between the proximity of academic sessions to flights. That said, the wing continues to schedule crews through as much academic study as is possible before their first flight.

Once a crew goes to the flight line, they fly a set number of sorties as part of their transition from ground-based training to flying, five for a WSO and six for a pilot. Interestingly, transition is the only phase of the course that comprises a different number of flights for the pilot and WSO. The pilot's sixth flight is an instrument check. If passed, the pilot is then cleared to be the aircraft commander without the need for another pilot onboard. All transition phase flights are flown with an instructor pilot and introduce the students to the basic aspects of the aircraft systems, instruments, and formation flying.

All Strike Eagles have controls in both the front and aft cockpits, so almost everything can be input and commanded from either cockpit, including take-off and landing if required.

That said, there are some limitations. The officer in the front seat has the only handle with which to lower the landing gear, but in an emergency the officer in the aft seat can blow down the landing gear.

The officer in the aft seat has limited straight ahead visibility which means they have to use peripheral vision during landing. (All instructor pilots are qualified to do this.) The officer in the aft seat cannot fire the M61 Vulcan cannon for the same reason.

The aircraft can be flown from either cockpit which has its benefits in the training context, as the student can shadow the controls as the instructor pilot walks them through the mechanics of the manoeuvre being attempted.

Basic fighter manoeuvres

There are six further phases to the course staged in the following order, as explained by the former commander of the 333rd Fighter Squadron, Lt Col Jonathan Bott.

"It starts off with offensive basic fighter manoeuvres [three sorties] where we park a bandit [positively identified enemy aircraft] in front of them and they learn how to employ air-to-air missiles and use HOTAS [the core controls of a fighter aircraft] to get manoeuvrability out of the jet at both high and low speeds. They transition to defensive BFM [three sorties] where we park the bandit behind them and they start to use the defensive systems on the jet, working together as a crew in order to manoeuvre the jet and survive, or ideally to turn the tables on the bandit.

"We complete a further two sorties designed to train them to use the vertical element, think in three dimensions, and gain a real understanding of the energy that is on their jet and how to use it as a weapon. The goal here, which is often misconstrued, is for them to understand the manoeuvrability on the aircraft and to be able to apply it in any scenario that they're going to face later on. Time spent in a part-task trainer helps a crew to learn how to work together, use tactical crew co-ordination, and use all of the avionic systems on the aircraft in order to employ it in more of a tactical scenario."

Basic air combat manoeuvring

"Air combat manoeuvring [ACM] is split into two phases, basic and advanced. Basic ACM teaches them how to operate as a formation; the basic fighting element for the F-15. One sortie, sometimes two, is flown involving two blue air versus one red air, all within the visual range. The term blue air is used for the friendly F-15Es, while red air is used for enemy aircraft. Red air aircraft are usually contractor-operated A-4 Skyhawks, sometimes Air Force F-16s or Navy F/A-18s.

"The primary goal is to park the red air aircraft behind the blue air and have the blue air jets communicate about where red air is and then how to operate as a formation to reverse on red air and kill them. Once a fight is complete, such that red air has been killed, we want them to be able to get back together as a fighting formation and exit that area, or separate, as quickly as possible. It's regaining two-ship visual mutual support, what we call Blue 39. We want that to be a driving factor so in the future they are never going to leave a wingman alone. It's foundational for the rest of their air-to-air training.

"In this phase we want to keep the red air aircraft close by, so they don't enter into a beyond visual range engagement. We need them to learn how to deconflict from their flight lead, how to communicate

Below: **An F-15E Strike Eagle, assigned to the 4th Fighter Wing approaches the boom of a KC-135 Stratotanker over the Southeastern United States on July 9, 2025.** USAF/SSgt Tiffany Emery

across the formation, how to make sure that they're shooting at the red air aircraft and not a blue air jet. We also need to reinforce the use of all three dimensions so they don't just focus on what they can do laterally, but keep in mind other dimensions, be it through G, time, space, and energy to operate a powerful F-15."

Basic surface attack

"At the start of the basic surface attack phase they've learned to work together as a crew, and how to work together as a formation. Now we teach them the basics of the air-to-ground mission set which represents 80% of what the F-15E is tasked to undertake. We also introduce low altitude operations and train them on a baseline selection of weapons at the beginning of this phase. Specifically, the 500lb GBU-12 laser-guided bomb, the 500lb GBU-38, and the 2,000lb GBU-31 GPS-guided JDAMs [Joint Direct Attack Munitions].

"The first two sorties are flown at medium altitude, teaching the crew how to employ GPS or laser-guided munitions and how to do so as a formation. Because F-15E crews must think about both offensive and defensive mission sets, we also start to train basic threat reactions, those used against older surface-to-air and man portable systems, so they learn how the jet performs at medium altitude.

"The next two sorties are flown to a weapons range where the crew uses the same employment functions as medium altitude, but now at low-level. The two sorties also introduce strafing. Three further sorties involve low altitude step down training, the first down to 1,000ft, then down to 500ft as a single ship, then down to 500ft as a formation, including tactical intercepts against another aircraft. During this phase our focus is getting them to understand the feel of the aircraft and how to work together as a crew and as a formation at low altitudes."

Advanced air combat manoeuvring

"This phase returns to the air-to-air role because crews need to keep that as part of their mindset. We're trying to train them in multi-role operations. There's flexibility inherent in the aircraft, and we want them to keep thinking about one thing and then the other, not least because this phase leads into surface attack tactics, and the capstone events. To succeed in both they need to learn how to combine employing the F-15 in an air-to-air scenario with an air-to-ground scenario. This five-sortie phase furthers the knowledge of employing the aircraft, learning how to fight against another formation and transition to the visual range kill should special instructions and requirements dictate. Typically, two blue air versus two red air aircraft.

"They also learn how to respond defensively in an air-to-air scenario. Because we include tactics in a beyond visual range scenario with the understanding that a red air aircraft is going to cut loose from the fight, they have to be able to identify the red air aircraft that's still alive, where they're going in the airspace, change the geometry of their flight, talk between the formation, with one of them defending while the other is cleaning up the red air aircraft still at large. It really makes them think and work, which we want them to do in each tactical event that, on average, lasts between two and three minutes. Then we set up the next engagement.

"Three further sorties involve tactical intercepts within a beyond visual range scenario with two blue air versus a minimum of two, but ideally four red air aircraft. This allows us to paint different pictures and different geometric considerations for their intercepts. By the end of the ACM phase, provided everything has gone well, they should achieve the majority of their air-to-air kills and solve the tactical problems given to them."

Advanced surface attack

"In the advanced phase of surface attack, we want them to be familiar with using the Sniper targeting pod. We also want them to be familiar with and have regular crosschecks of the Link-16 data link and the aircraft's defence systems. This phase comprises three sorties. The first two are flown to a weapon range so they can gain weapons currency or unfinished weapons qualifications. On at least one of the two sorties, we load a minimum of eight 500lb bombs for heavy munition employment. Then we qualify them on the weapons mentioned earlier. We also train them to use the low altitude terrain-following radar and employ weapons using that radar.

"The third sortie is a capstone event designed to drive home the necessity of good mission planning and involves multiple attacks in a variety of scenarios including close air support with Joint Terminal Attack Controllers."

Above: **F-15E Strike Eagles assigned to the 4th Fighter Wing parked on the flightline at Travis Air Force Base, California, during Exercise Bamboo Eagle 24-3.** USAF/Capt Benjamin Aronson

Surface attack tactics

"This two-sortie phase includes dynamic targeting which typically involves crews working with a dedicated command and control agency. This first sortie also introduces crews to maritime strike warfare and involves hunting for specific boats or targets along the Atlantic coast. The second sortie is dedicated to destruction of enemy air defences. It is designed to drive home the need to understand the types of threat they may face in an air-to-ground environment, and how to deal with such threats using the variety of weapons the crew can bring to bear.

"Crews complete the course with two capstone sorties. Each one is designed by the squadron's weapon officers and are based on the needs of operational squadrons at the time. Typically, these involve a scenario in which the crews have to employ the aircraft in both the air-to-air and the air-to-ground roles in the same sortie. They must mix the two roles and go

through a phase-based approach of how to tactically win each scenario."

Crew performance

The F-15E B-course presents all student pilots and WSOs with a highly saturated learning environment. Bott explained: "The purpose of the course is to build stress on the crews who must demonstrate the flexibility of mind and intellectual curiosity required to understand that what they do today may not be what they do tomorrow, and that being prepared is key. In any week of the course a crew might learn about aspects of the air-to-ground role one day, while flying air-to-air sorties the following day, and during the same week take tests on systems they've yet to use in a jet. By the end of the course, the vast majority of them have figured out what they individually need to do to be successful in their day-to-day study habits, time management, and how to improve upon their areas of weakness.

"We help them in a number of ways. First, we speak with their families both at the beginning of the course and as the student approaches the difficult phases, to explain what's happening. We outline what the family needs to be prepared for at home and the ways they can get support from the 4th Fighter Wing, making sure they know we are here to help. Each student is assigned a mentor, one of our instructor pilots or WSOs who gets to know the student and guides them through the difficult phases. Also, we assign groups of four students to a flight commander, a senior instructor, typically a Captain, someone with the ability to control their schedule and organise meetings with any of the squadron's staff to help with their needs.

"On average, about 15% of student crews would struggle to make it through the course if these measures were not in place. For those that are struggling, we put them on special monitoring status, and then only fly them with the most capable and senior instructors. We also organise their schedule with necessary study time built in and provide extra help to get them across the line. Today we're averaging a loss of one to two aviators per class, usually due to a shortfall in aptitude to the course. When that happens, they are reclassed into a different aircraft.

"Those that graduate attend a ceremony on a Friday and by Monday morning they'll start duty at one of the two operational squadrons based at Seymour Johnson to start three months of mission qualification training, which is an introduction to the different mission sets flown by their squadron. Those posted to Mountain Home or Lakenheath face a two- or three-week break in training to move and get checked in."

Each F-15E FTU is budgeted for a 5,700-hour flying programme per year. Currently, the two F-15E FTUs are tasked with training 48 crews (96 officers) a year, a slightly higher number than in recent years to address the fighter pilot shortage faced by the Air Force over the past five years.

Decorations for combat

On March 28, 2025, airmen assigned to the 4th Fighter Wing were awarded high-level decorations by Gen Ken Wilsbach, then commander of Air Combat Command, during a ceremony at Seymour Johnson Air Force Base. The airmen were recognised for their rapid response and performance in the largest air-to-air engagement in over 50 years.

In April 2024, airmen assigned to the 335th Expeditionary Fighter Squadron (EFS) and 335th Expeditionary Fighter Generation Squadron deployed in support of US Central Command. Less than 24 hours after their arrival, multiple one-way attack drones and ballistic missiles were launched at Israel from Iran and Houthi-controlled regions of Yemen. Both units and coalition forces worked rapidly to defend Israel and counter the aerial attack.

From the evening of April 12 into the morning of April 13, 2024, 335th EFS aircrews successfully engaged and destroyed more than 80 one-way attack drones and at least six ballistic missiles. Thirty-one airmen were decorated for their actions including eight Distinguished Flying Crosses, one Bronze Star Medal, 12 Commendation Medals, and ten Air and Space Achievement Medals.

SENSITIVE
RECONNAISSANCE OPERATIONS

Based at Beale Air Force Base, California, the 9th Reconnaissance Wing is the only operator of the venerable U-2S high-altitude reconnaissance aircraft.

TWENTY YEARS AFTER pilot Gary Powers became headline news worldwide when his aircraft was shot down over central Russia in 1960, the name U-2 was still synonymous with everything bad about intelligence gathering. Consequently, when the US Air Force wished to reopen the production line to construct a version dedicated to battlefield surveillance in Europe, senior personnel considered it prudent to allocate an alternative designation.

Lockheed understood that it was sensible to build new aircraft for the task rather than develop unmanned aerial vehicles. An order was placed for 37 aircraft in November 1979, using existing jigs and tooling, but constructed at Palmdale, California. The majority were to become the TR-1, although some retained the U-2 designation despite an identical external appearance.

First to roll-out from the Palmdale line was TR-1A 80-1066 on July 15, 1981,

Right: **Pilots 'Ultralord' and 'Jethro' celebrate after landing a TU-2S at Beale Air Force Base, on August 1, 2025, following a flight on the 70th anniversary of the U-2's first flight.** USAF/SrA Frederick Brown

Below: **TU-2S 80-1078/BB lands at Beale Air Force Base, California, on August 1, 2025, following a mission that took place on the 70th anniversary of the U-2's first flight and broke the endurance records for the U-2, flying longer than 14 hours and travelling over 6,000nm.** USAF/ SrA Frederick Brown

with delivery to Beale in September. Eight were designated U-2Rs, one a U-2R(T) dedicated to training, two as ER-2s for the National Aeronautics and Space Administration, two TR-1B trainer versions, and the remaining 24 as operational TR-1A versions.

TR-1A 80-1068 was the first to visit Europe, arriving on August 30, 1982, for display at the Farnborough Air Show. It was hoped to generate export orders, possibly including the UK and Germany, although no further interest was forthcoming.

Earlier, the decision had been made to station TR-1s at RAF Alconbury in the UK, where the 17th Reconnaissance Wing (RW) and its flying component, the 95th Reconnaissance Squadron (RS), both activated on October 1, 1982. The wing was accountable to Strategic Air Command's 7th Air Division, with headquarters at Ramstein Air Base, West Germany, which organised day-to-day tasking on behalf of United States Air Forces in Europe.

The first pair of TR-1As, 80-1068 and 80-1070, was delivered to Alconbury during February 1983, and because the TR-1 was capable of assuming the intelligence gathering duties and its own battlefield tasking, the U-2R assigned to Detachment 4 at RAF Mildenhall ceased operations. Consequently, the final resident U-2R, 68-10337, returned to Beale.

Also in the UK, RAF Mildenhall's association with the U-2 began in June 1977, based on short-term visits, but changed to a full-time basis on March 30, 1979, when 68-10338 arrived.

TR-1A deliveries to Alconbury were slow, largely because the aircraft's dedicated sensors were being developed at a somewhat leisurely pace. Missions were quite often flown to West Germany and the Baltic Sea area to monitor the traditional Warsaw Pact nations, with sorties lasting up to nine hours.

Thirteen huge, hardened aircraft shelters were constructed by 1989, with roughly

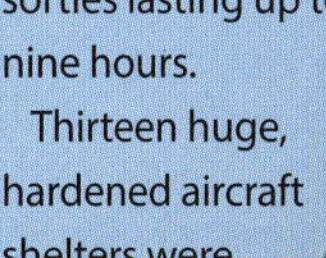

that number of aircraft assigned. As new sensors, including the Precision Location Strike System and the ASAR-2, were developed, aircraft were either retrofitted at Alconbury, or during Programmed Depot Maintenance at the Warner Robins Air Logistics Center in Georgia.

The end of the Cold War lessened the need for a TR-1 force in Europe. Consequently, the Alconbury-based 95th RS became a direct reporting unit to the 9th Strategic Reconnaissance Wing and the 17th RW was inactivated on June 30, 1991. Its assigned aircraft began to depart in August 1991. Half the fleet had left the Cambridgeshire base by the year end.

In October 1991, all the surviving TR-1As were redesignated as U-2R aircraft. The deteriorating situation in the Balkans required regular monitoring, with the 95th RS supporting a temporary assignment of a Beale-based U-2 equipped with the Senior Span system at Naval Air Station Sigonella, Sicily, in April 1992.

Later that year, the same jet deployed to Aviano Air Base, Italy. However, neither facility was ideally suited for supporting missions over the Balkans, so subsequent sorties were flown from Alconbury.

Below: **Pilots assigned to the 1st Reconnaissance Squadron prepare to taxi in a TU-2S aircraft at Beale Air Force Base on December 20, 2020.** USAF/SSgt Ramon Adelan

The 95th RS was inactivated on September 15, 1993, with its subsequent activities falling under Operating Location-United Kingdom (OL-UK). This enabled sorties to be undertaken with temporary duty personnel. RAF Alconbury was reduced to reserve base status, and on March 15, 1995, the remaining three aircraft relocated to RAF Fairford, the new temporary home for OL-UK. To this day, the Gloucestershire base continues to host U-2 operations, and supports transit flights between the United States, RAF Akrotiri, Cyprus, and the Middle East.

Beale, altitude and sensors

The 9th RW based operates the otherworldly U-2S Dragon Lady, a high-demand/low-density aircraft equipped with modular sensor and data link systems providing flexibility and mission essential intelligence, surveillance, and reconnaissance (ISR) to the combatant commands, joint and combined forces, and the intelligence community in peacetime and wartime.

Operating at altitudes over 70,000ft, the U-2 is an all-out reconnaissance aircraft. It provides critical imagery to meet the intelligence needs of the US national command authority and combatant commanders during peacetime or any phase of conflict. Intelligence data is gathered by three primary sensors referred to as ASARS, SYERS and ASIP, and Senior Span and Senior Spur satellite datalink systems.

The U-2S supports core missions such as Sensitive Reconnaissance Operations supporting the National Defense Strategy, in addition to other missions that include execution of combatant commander's operational plans, humanitarian assistance/disaster response (HADR), and to counter violent extremist organisations. The wing flies over 140,000 hours and 3,000 flights annually, including over 21,000 operational/combat sorties directed by the US Secretary of Defense and the Joint Chiefs of Staff.

The 9th Operations Group (OG) comprises the 1st and 99th Reconnaissance Squadrons; the 1st trains U-2 aircrew and the 99th conducts U-2 operations worldwide.

Explaining the U-2's primary sensors, Major Kelly, a U-2 pilot with the 9th Operations Support Squadron, said: "ASARS, or the Advanced Synthetic Aperture Radar Sensor, uses radar energy to create an image of the target, making it an all-weather, day or night sensor. SYERS, or Senior Year Electro-Optical Reconnaissance System, is an electro-optical/infrared imaging sensor that takes images in the visible and infra-red spectrum to capture enhanced literal images. ASIP, or Airborne Signals Intelligence Payload, is the standard signals intelligence sensor that collects and analyses electronic signals emitted from a wide variety of targets.

Above: **Pilots 'Ultralord' and 'Jethro' pose with all the members who made their U-2 70th anniversary flight possible, including from the 9th Reconnaissance Wing, 1st Reconnaissance Squadron, 9th Physiological Support Squadron, and 9th Aircraft Maintenance Squadron, on August 1, 2025.** USAF/SrA Frederick Brown

"The U-2 employs at unmatched operational altitudes, which equates to unmatched sensor ranges from an airborne asset. This combination allows the U-2 to see further than any other airborne asset, and quickly adjust collection based on real-time circumstances."

Kelly said the importance of ISR as a capability is twofold: "Before hostilities commence, ISR provides and updates the orders of battle that planners rely upon to understand the adversary and prepare for combat. Once combat operations begin, ISR is essential to finding, fixing, tracking, targeting, and assessing targets. ISR is the essential thread that finds, keeps custody of, and develops targets, and then judges how successfully the target was engaged."

Exercising readiness

The 9th RW regularly undertakes exercises to evaluate its readiness such as Dragon Fang, a full-scale readiness exercise designed to test the wing's ability to rapidly deploy and perform mission essential tasks while in a mock deployed setting. The end goal of the exercise was to prepare the wing to transition to the new Air Force Force Generation (AFFORGEN) deployment model.

Col Geoffrey Church, 9th RW commander, explained the purpose of the exercise was to test and evaluate the wing's ability to survive and operate during combat operations. The week-long exercise involved 13 units

assigned to the 9th RW, California Air National Guard's 195th Wing, and A Company of California Army National Guard's 140th Security and Support Aviation Battalion.

Technical Sergeant Channon Green, 9th RW wing inspection planner, said: "The purpose of Dragon Fang is to evaluate and prepare us for the AFFORGEN model and to ensure that the 9th RW can give what is requested of them effectively, efficiently, and on time."

Airmen faced multiple tests of events that would lead up to a contested environment. Some of these events included airstrikes, ground assaults, chemical, biological, radiological, and nuclear events, and triage capabilities.

Airmen were inspected on their ability to accomplish required mission essential tasks (METs) involving these scenarios. Capt Miles Bliss, 9th RW director of inspections, said: "An example of one of the METs we were testing was the ability to perform PAR [post attack reconnaissance] sweeps, so searching for UXOs [unexploded ordnance] post attack and making sure that the base was clear, doing recovery operations to check for damage to buildings and runways, and start repairs on them."

Members of the 9th Security Forces Squadron pulled airmen from different units to provide constant base defence while simultaneously being attacked,

Left: **Major William, U-2 pilot with the 99th Expeditionary Reconnaissance Squadron, steers U-2S 80-1087/BB to a parking spot after completing his 100th combat mission in the U-2.** USAF/MSgt Jennifer Calhoun

Below: **U-2S Dragon Lady 80-1070/BB flies over the Golden Gate Bridge near San Francisco on a photo mission from Beale Air Force Base, about 130 miles to the northeast of the city.** USAF/SSgt Robert Trujillo

and provided the first line of response to these events.

Capt Ricky Sizemore, 9th Security Forces Squadron operations officer, said: "With this exercise, we implemented multi-capable airmen to fulfil force protection and security forces roles. This helps us build up a heightened defence posture and allows for more people to be in the fight."

The attacks resulted in injuries and casualties, but medical technicians assigned to the 9th Medical Group quickly triaged patients based on the level of care needed, implemented Tactical Combat Catastrophe Care, and handled mortuary affairs.

Airmen from different agencies collaborated in the emergency operations centre to advise wing leadership on how to effectively employ the proper support needed to respond to the scenarios while still executing the mission.

Deployment support

The 9th Logistics Readiness Squadron (LRS) Individual Deployment Readiness Cell (IDRC) has an assigned team of airmen and civilians comprising logistics planners, force support personnel, and an installation deployment officer who provides overall daily command and control for Beale's deployment process, and stands up as the Deployment Control Center (DCC) during large exercises or mass deployments.

Controlling movements, travel, supplies and making sure people get to their destination and back safely, is a lengthy and daunting task. Explaining, a deployment operations officer said: "An effective deployment machine is mainly accomplished through a combined effort with unit deployment managers as we guide them throughout the process of pre-deployment preparation and ongoing maintenance of individual level readiness."

The deployment operations officer explained that Beale has a unique mission: "Our aircraft have a permanent presence in specific locations and our requirements are not swapped out with another wing at the end of a rotation, such as with fighters. This requires our personnel to maintain a high level of readiness year-round."

DCGS Distributed Surface Asset

Based at Beale Air Force Base (AFB), California, the 548th Intelligence, Surveillance, and Reconnaissance Group (ISRG) comprises four active-duty squadrons, two Air Force Reserve Command squadrons, two California Air National Guard squadrons, along with a geographically separated detachment at Davis-Monthan AFB, Arizona.

The 9th Intelligence Squadron (IS) conducts analysis and processing, exploitation, and dissemination (PED)

Above: **A U-2 pilot drives a high-performance chase car down the runway to catch a U-2 performing a low touch and go at Al Dhafra Air Base, UAE. The pilot driving the chase car helps the pilot flying the U-2 by communicating alignment with and height above the runway during take-offs and landings.** USAF/SrA Gracie Lee

Propulsion shop

The U-2's GE Aviation F118-GE-101 engine is maintained at the 9th RW by the 9th MXS aerospace propulsion shop with responsibility for the flightline maintenance, ensuring serviceability after every flight, conducting oil analysis, and any time-based maintenance.

Master Sergeant Byron Johnson, a flight chief with the 9th MXS said: "Working on the U-2 engine is unique. Unlike other aircraft that allow for relatively easy access to the engine, we have to disassemble it and pull off the entire back half of the aircraft, changing filters and constantly looking the engine over to keep it running smoothly. We find small things occasionally, that if neglected could lead to bigger problems later. Sometimes, if the engine doesn't come out for a little while, a small problem could manifest itself into something bigger, so it is important we address it right away."

Fuel systems

Maintenance of the U-2's fuel components are the responsibility of the 9th MXS's aircraft fuel systems specialists. "When the aircraft come down and the crew chiefs see a fuel leak or an issue with one of our components, they'll call us out to evaluate the leak or troubleshoot the issue. Knowing the aircraft and how our parts work allows us to troubleshoot different possibilities and narrow it down to the exact problem. For instance, a boost pump's pressure read out is supposed to be 10 to 20PSI," said Senior Airman Steven Benton, a fuels systems technician with the 9th MXS.

One important task for the aircraft fuel systems shop is maintaining the hydrazine and emergency start system. Explaining, Staff Sergeant Kirk Smith, 9th MXS aircraft fuel systems craftsman, said: "The emergency start system is a onetime chance to restart the engine if something goes wrong during flight. To work on it, we must be certified to work with hydrazine."

Aircrew flight equipment

Specialists assigned to the aircrew flight equipment shop of the 9th Operations Support Squadron are responsible for ensuring pilots' equipment is up to date and safe for use.

"We inspect and maintain their gear regularly to ensure all their equipment is in perfect working condition," said Airman 1st Class Joshua Chatman. When inspecting or maintaining equipment, a pilot's safety is the number one priority, and for that reason aircrew flight equipment specialists use the Defense Property Accountability System (DPAS). Details of all inspections and maintenance conducted on flight equipment are input to the system, with a weekly run through of the flight's overdue list to make sure nothing has been missed.

Oxygen masks, oxygen tanks, parachutes, G-suits, helmets, and survival kits are just a portion of the variety of equipment maintained by the aircrew flight equipment shop.

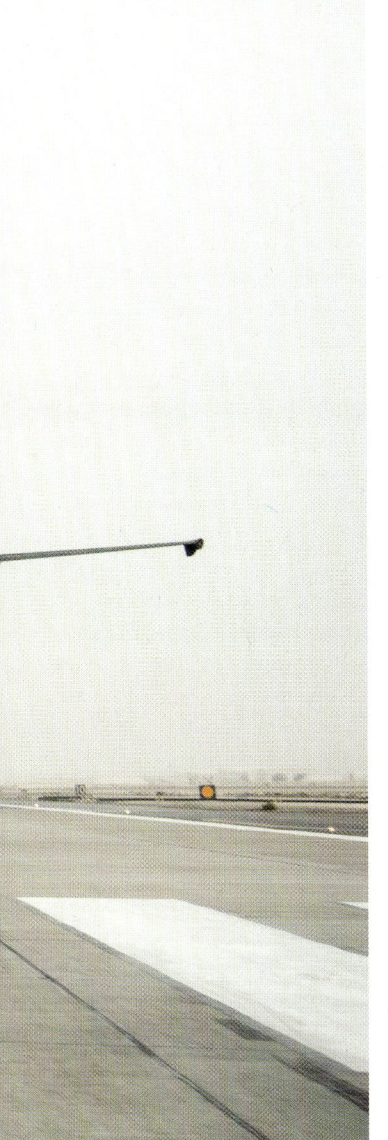

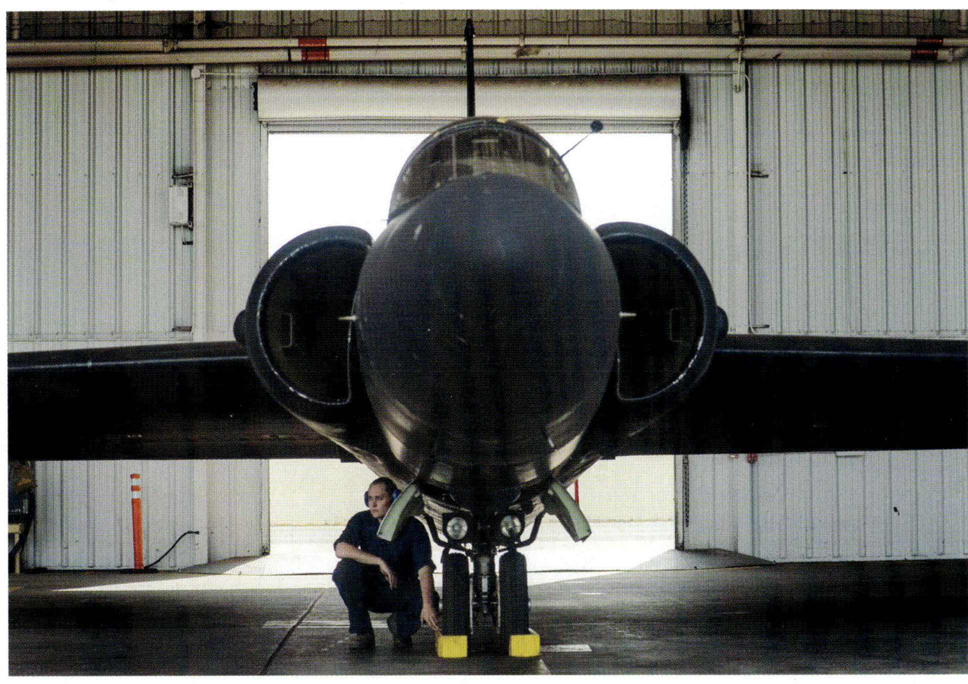

Above: **An aircraft maintainer completes the final inspection of a U-2S before pilots taxi the aircraft out of the hangar to the runway at Beale Air Force Base.** USAF/SSgt Kenny Holston

Egress systems

Ejection is a pilot's last chance at survival. Their lives rest in the hands of aircrew egress system specialists assigned to 9th MSX who inspect, maintain and service all aircraft exit systems installed on U-2, TU-2 and T-38 aircraft assigned to the 9th RW, to ensure they are functioning properly.

Discussing the work, Staff Sergeant Cody Clark, 9th MXS aircrew egress craftsman, said: "We try to schedule anywhere from two to three seats in a typical week, and that's not including unscheduled maintenance that could pop up. The work has no margin for error. Airmen at the egress shop rely on each other to make sure the job gets done. But I feel confident knowing that our crew executed everything perfectly because we do not settle for anything less than perfection."

Petroleum, oil and lubricants

Liquid Oxygen (LOX) called Aviator's Breathing Oxygen (ABO) is a pilot's main

Left: **A pilot steers a U-2S to its parking spot while being marshalled by a crew chief. The aircraft is assigned to the 99th Expeditionary Reconnaissance Squadron at Al Dhafra Air Base, United Arab Emirates.** USAF/MSgt Jennifer Calhoun

engines: both NASA ER-2s, all four TU-2S trainer and 31 U-2S aircraft.

The U-2S remains the US Air Force's only manned, strategic, high-altitude, long-range ISR platform, capable of signals intelligence (SIGINT), imagery intelligence (IMINT) – the new name for photography – and measurement and signature intelligence (MASINT) collection.

Intelligence gathering requires sensors and the U-2S can carry some of the most advanced devices ever produced. These can be installed in a variety of interchangeable noses, and within slipper tanks positioned on both wings. These can carry a wide variety of advanced optical, multispectral, synthetic aperture radar, SIGINT, and other payloads simultaneously. Sensor bays permit rapid installation of new equipment to counter emerging threats and requirements.

U-2s comprise half of the high-altitude ISR fleet and are heavily tasked. Recent improvements to Block 20 configuration feature a glass cockpit, digital autopilot,

source of air at altitudes exceeding 10,000ft and it is paramount to U-2 pilots and the mission. In the 9th RW, LOX is provided by airmen assigned to the 9th LRS and fuels cryogenics technicians who work with Petroleum, Oil and Lubricants (POL).

Fuels cryogenics technicians don white personal protective equipment to ensure they are safe while handling LOX and performing tests. Airman 1st Class Randy Willis, a 9th LRS cryogenics technician said: "We wear specialised protective gear to prevent our skin from burns because the LOX is pressurised gas at -297°F [-182°C]. After servicing and testing, the LOX is delivered to and put into the aircraft for the pilots to use."

Aerospace ground equipment

To support U-2 maintenance and flying operations at Beale, the 9th MXS aerospace ground equipment (AGE) flight inspects, maintains, modifies, and repairs all aerospace ground equipment that supplies electricity, hydraulic pressure, and air pressure to the wing's assigned aircraft.

The AGE flight, which is responsible for over 500 pieces of equipment, is divided into four different sections: maintenance performs major fixes, inspection does preventative maintenance, minor fixes and service, while delivery deliver the equipment to the requesting units, and support provides the tools needed to fix equipment.

Current configuration

Pratt & Whitney's J75 engine had powered the U-2 since its earliest days, but developments in design enabled the more powerful and lighter General

Above: **Col James Bartran, 9th Reconnaissance Wing deputy commander, greets Major Matthew, 99th Reconnaissance Squadron chief of expeditionary operations upon the completion of the final flight of U-2S 80-1085 on April 5, 2024, at Beale Air Force Base. Aircraft 1085's final flight was completed from Joint Base Pearl Harbor-Hickam, Hawaii, to Beale.** USAF/A1C Colin Smith

Right: **A U-2 pilot rests prior to a mission from RAF Fairford in Gloucestershire.** USAF/SrA Eugene Oliver

Right: **A U-2 pilot receives suit preparations prior to a mission flown from RAF Fairford.** USAF/ SrA Eugene Oliver

Electric F118-GE-F29 to be installed for the first time in May 1989. This was a difficult integration. Protracted trials and delayed funding prevented F118 engines from entering service until October 1994, with the aircraft then designated as the U-2S and TU-2S. Thirty-seven aircraft received F118

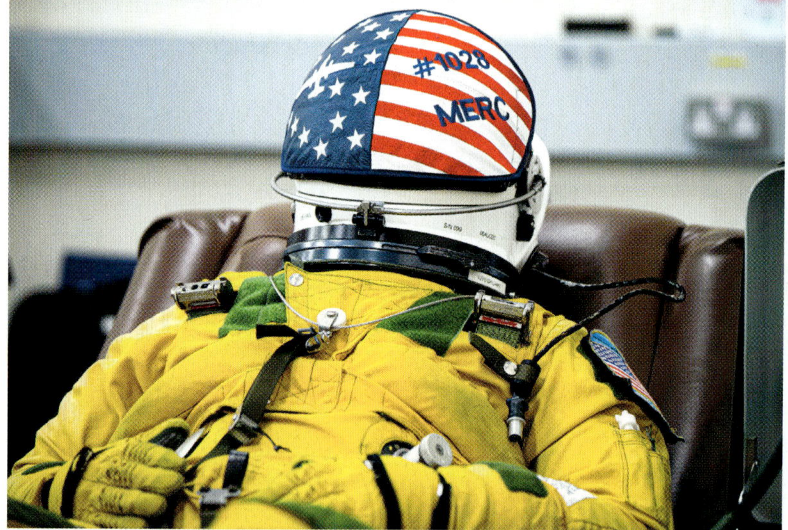

NOTABLE U-2S EVENTS

On March 25, 2023, a U-2S Dragon Lady and airmen assigned to the 9th RW, based at Beale AFB, deployed to Offutt AFB, Nebraska for Exercise Dragon Flag East.

The exercise was staged to further prepare the 9th RW for potential agile combat employment (ACE) operations around the world to meet combatant commanders' objectives and in accordance with the National Defense Strategy. ACE is a proactive and reactive operational scheme of manoeuvre executed within threat timelines to increase survivability while continuing to generate combat power despite enemy attempts at saturation attacks on forward airfields.

During Dragon Flag East, airmen executed collaborative reconnaissance missions using the U-2S and RC-135 Rivet Joint aircraft based at Offutt to provide adaptable, agile combat support to the combatant command. This involved working with the 55th Wing's multi-capable airmen (MCA) cell to advance cross-utilisation of their core career specialties.

Col Kristen Thompson, 55th Wing commander, said: "The effort is designed to improve how we collect, analyse, and share information and make operational decisions more effectively than our potential adversaries, and increases our survivability in a contested environment."

In September 2023, Lockheed Martin Skunk Works completed the first flight of the first test phase of a U-2 fitted with systems integrated under the U-2's Avionics Tech Refresh (ATR) programme following the contract award in 2020. Systems included an updated avionics suite, a new mission computer designed to the USAF's OMS standard that enables the U-2 to integrate with systems across air, space, sea, land, and cyber domains at disparate security levels, and new modern cockpit displays.

The FY2025 budget year is the final year that the air force will maintain operational capability of the U-2 platform. Procurement funds are required, however, to sustain National Defense Authorization Act (NDAA)-directed capability and capacity, as well as safe and effective operations for the remainder of U-2's scheduled service.

Previously programmed funds have been shifted to support ASARS-2C procurement and fielding, which will enable vastly improved collection against emerging threats in the remainder of scheduled U-2 operations.

Between June 3-6, the 9th RW conducted Exercise Ready Dragon to test the wing's ability to rapidly deploy and support operations in accordance with the ACE concept of operations in preparation for the wing's upcoming deployment cycle.

Explaining the exercise, Maj Matt Pianalto, 9th RW A3 Chief of Operations, said: "A wing operations centre, modelled after ACE principles, was set up to exercise the command-and-control function of establishing an air base that can expand its operation in the simulated United States Indo-Pacific Command Area-of-Responsibility."

Airmen faced scenarios designed to test their responses in a contested environment. Events included airstrikes, ground assaults, chemical, biological, radiological, and nuclear events, communication failures, landing zone installation manoeuvres and pararescue missions. Airmen were assessed by members of the Wing Inspection Team on their ability to accomplish mission essential tasks involving these scenarios.

Developing improvised landing zones is essential for missions that are geographically separated from the flight line, which allow aircraft to safely operate in any region, despite the terrain. The exercise scenario tested the 9th RW's ability to cohesively deploy airmen post-attack, to assess and establish a landing zone, and launch aircraft, all within threat timelines.

Explaining, Master Sargeant Cameron Piontek, 9th Operations Support Squadron landing zone safety officer, said: "The threat of peer adversaries being able to reach our CONUS [continental US] bases with a kinetic strike is very real, and we have to consider the potential that our airfields and mission support facilities are vulnerable. Should something like this happen, we must have a way to get a team out on the airfield and assess what is usable and what is not, in order to launch our remaining aircraft and get them somewhere safe as soon as possible."

Supported by California Air National Guard's 129th Rescue Wing from Moffat Air National Guard Base, the 9th RW was able to conduct a rescue of a simulated downed U-2 pilot from the water.

On the evening of July 31, 2025, a TU-2S assigned to the 9th RW took off from Beale AFB to begin the longest single flight the platform had ever attempted, flying across all 48 contiguous states of the United States. The date was significant: the 70th anniversary of the U-2's accidental maiden flight in 1955 by test pilot Tony LeVier over Groom Lake, Nevada. The aircraft returned to Beale more than 14 hours later, having flown more than 6,000nm breaking endurance records for an aircraft of its class.

The aircraft was flown by aircrew from America's longest-serving flying unit, the 1st RS. The commander, Lt Col John Mattson, said: "The character of war is changing, but ownership of our mission to build aircrew ready to exploit and dominate the electromagnetic spectrum and win, will never change."

The pilots chosen were 1st RS assigned flight safety officer and U-2 instructor pilot, callsign 'Ultralord', and the 1st RS instructor pilot and U-2 chief pilot, callsign Jethro, who both hold records for the highest amount of U-2 flight hours. Commenting, 'Ultralord' said: "Eleven years ago, I realised just how far we could hypothetically fly the U-2 if we really wanted to push its limits to see just what it could it do. On the 70th anniversary of the U-2, '70 years at 70,000ft', it seemed right to demonstrate the true capability of this aircraft."

Such flights, however, remain hypothetical without precision mission planning to turn it into a reality. This involves planning and co-ordinating flight routes, choosing emergency refuelling stops and accounting for factors such as winds, temperatures, altitudes, and not crossing a border into the wrong air space.

This flight was also instrumental in improving the 1st RS's new mission planning software to plan for more complex missions. The software had not been used for a flight this long before, or with so many factors.

The 9th Physiological Support Squadron (PSPTS) provides the specialised support needed for U-2 pilots to fly at such daunting altitudes, such as maintenance of the pilots' protective high-altitude full pressure suits.

Technical Sergeant Christopher Burdi, 9th PSPTS assigned to the launch recovery team, said: "We already have to be perfect on every single flight, so with this one it just meant maintaining that standard of excellence. We had to ensure no incidents would occur for a longer flight than ever before, and that required more care, and more resources than usual."

The flight served to honour its 70-year legacy. It paid tribute to all those who had gone before and earned the privilege to be a member of the U-2 community. The Dragon Lady is one of the most difficult planes to fly due to its unique design, requiring a chase car to assist in landing. Just over 1,000 pilots have qualified to fly this aircraft, making it a tight-knit community.

As part of this tribute, the flight also honoured fallen U-2 pilots who made the ultimate sacrifice to their country by including specific flight paths over certain states, such as over the homes of these pilots' families. This was emphasised by 'Ultralord' after he touched down, noting the U-2 mission is only possible from the team efforts of all those serving today and all those who have come before.

"The incredible thing about this flight is that it shows not only the capabilities of the U-2, but that of our Air Force's most important asset, it's people," said Col Keagan McLeese, 9th RW commander. "Our Airmen demonstrated they are mission-ready in using the skills, adaptability and innovation it takes to generate global airpower."

Every June and December, US Air Force Weapons School based at Nellis AFB, Nevada, concludes its six-month Weapons Instructor Course designed to train weapons officers and enlisted technicians. Graduates advise at all levels of the US government, teach US Air Force leaders, and become experts of tactical and operational knowledge, authoring tactical doctrine.

The school graduates 150 students in each class. To earn the prestigious graduate patch, students must successfully complete the Weapons School Integration (WSINT). The course is staged for all weapon systems in service with the US Air Force, including the U-2S. Pilots who graduate from the course return to their operational squadron as an expert in the U-2 airframe and trained to integrate with other aircraft types to help prepare pilots to tactically employ the U-2 to achieve tactical, operational, and strategic level ISR effects in any peacetime or combat operation. During a WSINT, a team from the 9th RW support their pilots to find and fix priority targets to support the combat air forces' kill chain.

CURRENT COMBAT-CODED U-2S SQUADRONS

Squadron	Wing	Base	Major Command
1st RS	9th RW	Beale AFB, California	ACC
5th RS	9th RW	Osan AB, Republic of Korea	ACC
99th RS	9th RW	Beale AFB, California	ACC
Det 1 9th OG	9th RW	RAF Akrotiri, Cyprus	ACC
Det 3 9th OG	9th RW	RAF Fairford, England	ACC

Right: **A pilot guides a U-2 across Al Dhafra Air Base in the United Arab Emirates.** USAF/MSgt Jennifer Calhoun

modernised electronic warfare system, and updated data links.

Major sensors are Raytheon's ASAR-2A advanced synthetic aperture radar system, the UTC Aerospace SYERS-2A Senior Year electro-optical imagery system, and the enhanced ASIP airborne signals intelligence payload.

Data gathered is linked via satellite by the Senior Span and Senior Spur systems housed in a large elliptical radome atop the centre fuselage to ground stations for exploitation. The legacy optical bar camera system is also still used to provide broad-area imagery.

The fleet is currently undergoing upgrades to Block 20.1 standard, adding ASAR-2B, next-generation SIGINT, avionics and navigation improvements, with modernisation of the Link-16 datalink and the multi-function advanced datalink. ASAR-2B significantly improves the U-2 deep-look radar's ground mapping, moving target, and maritime modes.

Two ASAR-2B-equipped aircraft began flight testing in FY2022 and are expected to be fully operational by August, 2027. U-2S aircraft are also receiving stellar and GPS navigation, quick change modular mission systems, and upgrades of multispectral sensor and electronic warfare systems.

Airframe modifications, refreshing of helmet and pressure suits, and egress improvements are also ongoing. A host of contractors sustain the U-2. Lockheed Martin supports the airframes and much of the systems integration, while the following companies support and continue to enhance their sensor systems: Northrop Grumman (ASIP), Raytheon (ASAR), and UTC Aerospace (SYERS/Optical Bar Camera).

Unmanned aerial vehicles and satellites can perform most of the aircraft's mission functions. However, on each occasion the U-2 has proved to be more capable, and far more flexible than satellite and unmanned aerial systems. Under present arrangements, the U-2 has a guaranteed service life until at least 2027, but Lockheed Martin claims the airframes could fly until at least 2050.

Below: **A U-2 aircraft in a hangar at RAF Fairford. The aircraft supports a variety of missions that enhance regional and global security in support of US, NATO allies, and regional partners.** USAF/SrA Eugene Oliver

Beale AFB in northern California is home to the 9th RW and its component U-2 squadrons: the 1st RS as the formal training unit, and the 99th RS as the operational squadron. The 1st RS flies the TU-2S two-seat trainer, the U-2S and the T-38C Talon as a proficiency trainer.

Overseas, the 5th RS at Osan Air Base, Republic of Korea, monitors activities on the Korean peninsula, China, and eastern Russia. At RAF Akrotiri, Cyprus, Detachment 1 monitors North Africa and eastern Mediterranean nations, while the 99th Expeditionary Reconnaissance Squadron at Al Dhafra Air Base in the United Arab Emirates provides ISR missions across the Middle East and southwest Asia, and retains operational responsibility for U-2S operations at RAF Fairford.

Ongoing test and evaluation are performed by Det 2, 563rd Test and Evaluation Group at Beale, using aircraft from the host wing. Air Force Materiel Command's Warner Robins

Air Logistics Complex (ALC) at Robins AFB, Georgia, occasionally uses a U-2S for development work. The ALC also performs some Programmed Depot Maintenance and manages the work to be completed by Lockheed Martin at its Palmdale facility.

U-2S tech refresh

In September 2023, Lockheed Martin Skunk Works, in partnership with the US Air Force, completed the first flight of the U-2 Dragon Lady's Avionics Tech Refresh (ATR) programme. The first flight involved a low-altitude functional check flight to integrate new avionics, cabling, and software as part of the ATR contract, and included an updated avionics suite (communications, navigation, display, etc) that modernises the U-2's onboard systems to readily accept and use new technology.

A new mission computer is designed to the US Air Force's open mission systems (OMS) standard and enables the U-2 to integrate with systems across air, space, sea, land, and cyber domains at disparate security levels.

New modern cockpit displays make pilot tasks easier, while enhancing presentation of the data the aircraft collects to enable faster, better informed decisions.

The ATR's first flight marked a milestone in the U-2's modernisation efforts and its path to be the first fully OMS-compliant fleet. Further testing will solidify a mature software baseline before mission systems are introduced to ensure both functionality and interoperability to meet operational needs. The U-2 ATR contract, valued at $50m, was awarded by the US Air Force in 2020.

Left: **A pilot climbs into the cockpit of a U-2 aircraft while a physiology support technician helps transport his oxygen.** USAF/ SrA Eugene Oliver

WILD WEASELS

Based at Shaw Air Force Base, South Carolina, the Block 50 F-16C -equipped 20th Fighter Wing has been in the business of suppressing or destroying surface-to-air missiles since 1991. This section provides an insight into the Wing's mission, aircraft, and maintenance.

ONCE AT THE heart of America's two-wing F-111 force based in England during the Cold War, the 20th Fighter Wing (FW) is now based at Shaw Air Force Base (AFB) in South Carolina.

Today the 20th FW flies the multi-role Block 50 F-16C. Its primary mission is to suppress or destroy enemy surface-to-air missiles and emitters, a concept dubbed Wild Weasel.

Wild Weasel is the name given to those US Air Force aircraft specifically configured to destroy enemy radar and surface-to-air missile systems as part of the suppression of enemy air defences mission set. Project Wild Weasel was the US Air Force development plan for an aircraft dedicated to detecting, suppressing, and destroying surface-to-air missile systems, most notably those developed by the Soviet Union.

Today's dedicated Wild Weasel aircraft in US Air Force service is the Block 50 F-16C. This specially configured version of Lockheed Martin's F-16 Fighting Falcon is equipped with sensors, a targeting system, and the AGM-88 High-speed Anti-Radiation Missile (HARM).

The Block 50 F-16C is the fourth major design series type to perform the Wild Weasel role after the F-100 Super Sabre, F-105 Thunderchief, and F-4 Phantom. The Wild Weasel concept includes SEAD (Suppression of Enemy Air Defences) and DEAD (Destruction of Enemy Air Defences). SEAD is generally a non-kinetic temporary effect versus DEAD in which the target is kinetically destroyed.

Active-duty Block 50 F-16C squadrons are assigned to Misawa Air Base, Japan (two), Spangdahlem Air Base, Germany (two), and Shaw AFB (three). Shaw is home to the 20th FW with the 55th, 77th and 79th Fighter Squadrons assigned the 20th Operations Group (OG).

The primary Offensive Counter Air SEAD (OCA-SEAD) and DEAD roles performed by the Block 50 F-16C are only two of many types of mission conducted. Squadrons assigned to the 20th FW also undertake defensive counter air (DCA), offensive counter air-escort, close air support (CAS), maritime air support (MAS), and air defence.

The training flights required to maintain combat-ready proficiency in all the missions listed above are basic fighter manoeuvring, air combat manoeuvring, tactical intercepts, basic surface attack, aircraft handling characteristics (AHC), and instrument flying.

The first Wild Weasel Block 50 F-16, serial number 90-0801, rolled off the Fort Worth production line on October 31, 1991. The last of 181 Block 50 aircraft powered by General Electric F110-GE-129 engines, serial number 01-7053, was delivered to the US Air Force at Shaw on March 25, 2005. The air force also received 50 Block 52s powered by Pratt & Whitney F100-PW-229 engines.

The Block 50 F-16 is designed to shoot the AGM-88 High-speed Anti-Radiation Missile in the SEAD and DEAD roles. That capability forms the basis for all three squadrons assigned to the 20th FW.

Aircrew training

SEAD is a core mission for the 20th FW and requires all junior pilots to undergo a SEAD Flight Lead Upgrade (FLUG) sortie in which the student develops a game plan, leads the flight, executes the mission, and conducts part of the de-brief session.

An instructor pilot builds the scenario several days prior to the FLUG mission, followed by mission planning involving the student, the instructor, and any other pilots involved on the day before. Lasting about six hours, mission planning involves a 'chalk talk' when the pilots poke holes in the plan, query the student's intent, determine his level of understanding, and draw their attention

Below: **The 79th Fighter Squadron's flagship, F-16C 91-0379 flies over the Gulf of Mexico on November 8, 2021, during Checkered Flag 22-1.** USAF/SSgt Betty Chevalier

Above: **A crew chief assigned to the 380th Expeditionary Aircraft Maintenance Squadron, waits to marshal an F-16 assigned to the 79th Expeditionary Fighter Squadron in the US Central Command area of responsibility in February 2020.** USAF/SSgt Joseph Pick

to aspects they have not considered. This gives the student the chance to refer to the manuals and incorporate changes into their briefing for the mission the next day. This amounts to almost a full day of preparation for an hour-and-a-half sortie.

The scheduled brief lasts about an hour and half. Once pilots step to their aircraft, it's another hour before take-off. From landing, it takes another hour before the pilots are back in the building ready to start looking at the tapes, shot information, shot validation, and a determination of what the student did. This is followed by a meeting with red air for a de-brief. The student gets two-and-a-half hours to de-brief before the instructor takes to the podium to critique everything from start to finish and discuss the key aspects from which to learn, then what must be applied on the next mission. The entire process is designed make the student realise how much focus must be applied.

FLUG is one of ten upgrade programmes run by the squadrons assigned to the 20th FW. One example is the instructor pilot upgrade, (IPUG), which focuses on the responsibilities of overseeing a trainee and leading a formation safely. Another example is the mission commander qualification which allows a pilot to lead an entire strike package through the planning and the execution.

Pilots must also qualify on the AAQ-33 Sniper advanced targeting pod to ensure a full understanding of the system's complexities, as well as night vision goggles and their use when flying at low-level.

Other regular, but notable, training events conducted include surface-to-air and air-to-air threat reaction (executing the appropriate manoeuvre to try to break from a ground emitter targeting the aircraft with its radar and defeating the missile), use of chaff and flares, surface-to-air and air-to-air electronic attack, moving target attacks using either laser-guided bombs or precision-guided munitions, and strafing of moving targets.

Live, virtual and constructive

One construct now used by the 20th FW for local and large force exercise training programmes is LVC – the integration of live, virtual, and constructive assets.

During a presentation given at the Interservice/Industry Training, Simulation and Education Conference in Orlando, Florida, on December 3, 2014, Maj Gen James Jones, then Air Force assistant deputy chief of staff for operations, plans and requirements, said a Block 50 F-16 cost about $7,500 per flying hour, compared to $900 for an hour of LVC training. An attractive proposition for

mixing any of the 18 major design series aircraft in US Air Force service in large simulations integrated into a regional training event.

Mission planning

When planning a SEAD mission, pilots need to understand the combatant commander's intention otherwise the F-16 pilots can execute their mission on the wrong path. Starting with the enemy, the Wild Weasel pilots must get a clear understanding of the target, the defences around the target, what the enemy might do to counter the strike, and what aircraft and systems will be part of the strike package. Many of the answers are provided by the intelligence squadron.

The Wild Weasel pilots then devise a game plan and the subsets involved, for example, air-to-air. How will they get in the target area, and what happens if an enemy fighter pops up? On the air-to-ground side, how do the aircraft in the main strike package flow into the target, and do they have restrictions? Some weapons might need to be dropped from a certain profile, some munitions can be released and let go, others must be laser-designated on the target. That's important because it presents increased vulnerability times for the strikers.

The attack profile is important for a SEAD mission so the F-16C's ASQ-213

Left: **Airmen assigned to the 79th Fighter Generation Squadron at Joint Base Charleston, South Carolina on January 26, 2021, prepare to chock the incoming jet during an ACE training event.** USAF/ SSgt Destinee Sweeney

HARM Targeting System can detect and classify different emitters. Pilots spend a lot of time during the mission planning stage to try and manage all the different emitter frequencies to create a useful presentation in the cockpit. If they fail to achieve that, they must spend time manipulating the information and managing the beeps and squeaks.

As part of the game plan, decisions must be made about crucial aspects such as the system settings, countermeasures, weapon settings and radar channel to make it coherent. Wild Weasel pilots need to consider the problem set and what could happen. About 99.9% of the time the contracts are not executed as planned because the enemy does something that requires a dynamic response. As any threat can suddenly transmit information and light up, pilots must think very quickly during a SEAD mission.

New weapons and avionics

The latest weapons released to the Combat Air Forces used by the Block 50 F-16 are the GBU-39/B Small

Below: **F-16C 91-0372/ SW assigned to the 79th Expeditionary Fighter Squadron takes off from Palanquero Air Base near Rionegro, Colombia, during Exercise Relampago VI on July 15, 2021.** USAF/SrA Duncan Bevan

Diameter Bomb I (SDB I) and the ADM-160 Miniature Air Launched Decoy (MALD), and the latest avionics upgrade is the M7.0+ Operational Flight Program software.

Preparations for both new weapon or avionics are similar, leading up to receiving a system, the squadrons receive documentation giving the requirements for mission planning and pre-flight, and in the case of a munition, its employment.

The ADM-160 MALD has specific mission planning requirements that need dedicated training sessions. Pilots complete part-test training which involves simulated employment of the ADM-160 on a regular sortie to give the pilot a chance to interact and interface with the missile during a mission that does not require target acquisition or reaction to surface-to-air missiles. Once a pilot has gained familiarity with the ADM-160, their knowledge is incorporated into a tactical sortie.

The earlier M6.2 software load included an auto ground collision avoidance system (AGCAS). Pilots must learn about its activation and the software anomalies because there are times when it activates and should not have done so.

A subset called the Pilot Activated Recovery System (PARS) is activated by the pilot via a button if they become spatially disoriented, and the system recovers the aircraft. For familiarisation with PARS and to gain confidence in the systems, pilots fly a couple of profiles at given angles of attack, bank and air speed and hit the button to experience the PARS recover the aircraft.

Raytheon trophy winners

On August 6, 2021, Lt Col Cass, then commander of the 79th FS 'Tigers', and his squadron colleagues, were notified by the then 20th OG commander, who was the expeditionary wing commander for Red Flag, that the 79th had been named the top air dominance squadron in the US Air Force for its actions across five combat operations and two exercises during FY2020, and was the recipient of the Raytheon Trophy. The announcement was made at the end of the exercise Red Flag out brief at Nellis AFB, Nevada, in a room full of fighter pilots. "Given Nellis is home of the fighter pilot, that's a great place to be to find out," said Cass.

Originally started by the Hughes Aircraft Company in 1953, the Raytheon Trophy is awarded to the most outstanding air superiority squadron based on operational mission performance, exercise participation and inspection results, as well as unit and individual achievements.

While deployed to the US Central Command (CENTCOM) area of operations, the 'Tigers' helped improve partner nation interoperability through joint training opportunities and large force exercises. The squadron's decisive airpower ensured NATO and regional forces could focus on their missions while simultaneously protecting friendly forces

Right: **Two 79th Fighter Squadron F-16Cs head out to the Gulf Range Complex to shoot AIM-9 missiles on a mission during WSEP 22-2.** USAF/79th FS

in the region. The 79th Fighter Squadron (FS) was awarded the Gallant Unit Citation for its heroic actions after the squadron was able to launch jets for base defence less than 40 minutes after an attack on Bagram Air Base in Afghanistan.

Due to the COVID-19 pandemic, the 'Tigers' extended their deployment and helped ensure all air tasking orders were met while creating an innovative way to provide remote liaison support to the air operations centre. Following their redeployment, they focused on refining and upgrading their skills in support of all air-to-air and air-to-ground missions, concluding with a Combat Hammer air-to-ground weapons system evaluation programme (WSEP 20-12) at Hill AFB, Utah, where they were lauded for implementing lessons learned from their deployment to help their fellow training partners.

The 'Tigers' are the first active-duty F-16 squadron to win the Raytheon Trophy, and one of only three F-16 squadrons to take home the trophy since its inception in 1953. Commenting on his squadron's award, Cass expressed tremendous respect for the F-22 and the F-15 communities but said: "To have a unit that dropped many weapons against enemy forces and also worked with

Below: **F-16C 91-0372/SW flies over Colombia during Exercise Relampago VI on July 26, 2021.** USAF/SrA Duncan Bevan

Right: **An F-16C assigned to the 79th Fighter Squadron parked on the flight line at MacDill Air Force Base, Florida, on September 8, 2021. The squadron deployed to MacDill for an iteration of Exercise Raider Fires. The aircraft is loaded with a single 500lb GBU-54 LJDAM (on the right) and two 500lb GBU-12 laser-guided bombs (on the left).** USAF/A1C Hiram Martinez

friendly forces on the ground, redefines what it means to be the best fighter squadron in the US Air Force."

Cass and his colleagues were presented with the trophy on August 28, 2021, during a big party thrown by Raytheon attended by many of the pilots who had deployed to the CENTCOM area of responsibility in 2020 but had subsequently changed station.

Relampago in Colombia

The 20th FW regularly participates in Exercise Relampago with the Fuerza Aérea Colombiana at Palanquero Air Base, near the city of Rionegro, Colombia.

According to the 12th Air Force, airmen and pilots assigned to the 474th Expeditionary Operations Support Squadron (EOSS) and a fighter squadron, transformed a contingency location for conducting theatre training and joint, coalition and partnered missions during the exercise.

Flight operations included a mix of air-to-air and air-to-ground scenarios. Co-operative training included basic fighter manoeuvring and air combat manoeuvring to mirror real-world implications of maintaining regional security, with training sorties that focus on developing defensive counter air tactics and large force exercises.

Relampago's ongoing learning process led to opportunities for the 474th EOSS to derive strategy and implement previous home station training to conduct successful logistics operations working in tandem with the Fuerza Aérea Colombiana.

Airmen assigned to the 474th EOSS installed a mobile aircraft arresting system and transformed a small area of the Columbia Air Force's air base CACOM 5 for the preparation, launch, and recovery of combat training sorties of US Air Force F-16s and Fuerza Aérea Colombiana Kfir COA fighters assigned to Escuadrón de Combate 111.

Squadron Training

The AGM-88 HARM missile is the standard weapon of choice for doing SEAD. It allows an F-16 pilots to fly in a threat envelope and respond as the threat system lights the aircraft up, and for the pilot to shoot a HARM at the threat to allow the strikers and the bombers to get through.

Using a tongue in cheek but accurate comparison, Cass said: "I like to tell our guys that their job is to be a rodeo clown to go in, be seen, make noise and get shot at. That enables him to shoot back and allow the strikers to get through. In terms of the rodeo scenario, the strikers are the cowboys, we are professional rodeo clowns. Part of being a rodeo clown is being seen so the threat system targets you rather than the strikers. You react by shooting back. At a lot of our training focuses on how to do that, and the very deliberate tactics involved, all in a scenario that looks like chaos.

"When we shoot a HARM missile, one, we expect a need to do so. Two, we use sensors on the jet to be best postured to detect and geo locate the threat systems and to shoot a HARM. Alternatively, we might pass the location to another platform that can drop a precision-guided munition which might be one of the aircraft in our formation loaded with a GBU-54 or a GBU-38 to use against the threat to destroy it.

The author asked Cass how instructors introduce a junior pilot to the SEAD role given its, at least perceived, risky nature. The squadron boss said that one, instructors teach and stress the importance of reading and understanding the intelligence reports listing the threats and their capabilities. Explaining why, he said: "So you know when a radar and when a missile can reach out and get you. You must have that stuff down cold. You must know when you're in that threatened envelope. That's not the time to be looking down at your kneeboard card to see how many miles away the threat can hit you from. That requires a lot of self-studies and a lot of knowledge base which is all tailored into the day-to-day mission. There's a lot of self-studies in the days prior to the mission.

"Two, is knowing the capabilities of the F-16's weapons, knowing how to launch or shoot them, and when best to shoot a weapon so they achieve the required effect. Three, is knowing your threat reactions. Just because we're rodeo clowns doesn't mean we're going to go in and take punches. We know what ranges we can manoeuvre to abort, we know what radars are most susceptible

to different types of damage, and we know the manoeuvres required to defeat enemy radars for enemy missiles. And we'll perform jamming on top.

"Four, is teaching young pilots how to prioritise when they're in that environment of pure chaos, where to look, how to calmly communicate clearly, concisely, and correctly when they see certain threat parameters on their display, and then to execute the tasks of the flight lead's brief, so they don't have to be coached through the entire process. A lot of it comes down to priorities; taking a big problem and breaking it down into chunks and determining what's required."

Instruction of all the squadron's academic, simulator, mission qualification and flight lead training are specifically tailored to the SEAD mission set.

Discussing other aspects of the SEAD mission set, the author asked Cass about the co-operation between US Navy EA-18G Growlers and Wild Weasel F-16s during operations or at a Red Flag exercise. Cass said: "It's a close co-operative partnership. Any Wild Weasel flight or mission commander worth their salt will go find the Growler weapon instructor on the first day they

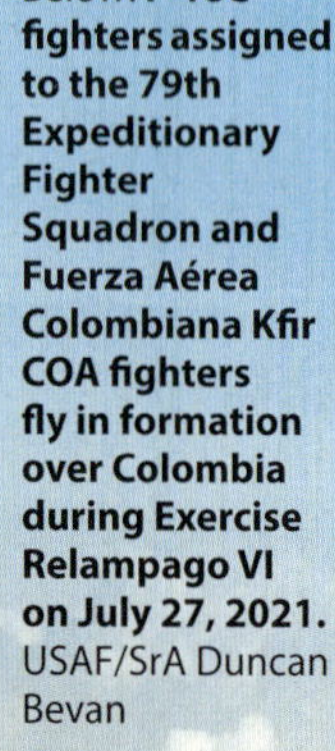

Below: **F-16C fighters assigned to the 79th Expeditionary Fighter Squadron and Fuerza Aérea Colombiana Kfir COA fighters fly in formation over Colombia during Exercise Relampago VI on July 27, 2021.** USAF/SrA Duncan Bevan

Fighter squadron and maintenance alignment

On April 1, 2021, Air Combat Command announced it was changing the structure of aircraft maintenance organisations to improve synchronisation between maintenance and fighter squadrons. The new Combat Oriented Maintenance Organization (COMO) is designed to flatten a maintenance organisation structure by transitioning an aircraft maintenance unit (AMU) into a fighter generation squadron (FGS).

An FGS is a new squadron comprised of maintainers responsible for aircraft health and sortie generation and will be paired with a fighter squadron such that the two units work collaboratively at home station and during deployments. Maj Gen Mark Slocum, Air Combat Command's director of air and space operations, said: "The benefit of this new organisational construct is to enhance the fighter force's agility and better prepares them for a future dynamic force employment in a high-end fight."

Maj Gen Tom Miller, Air Combat Command's director of logistics, engineering and force protection,

Above: An F-16C Fighting Falcon assigned to the 79th Fighter Squadron heads out to the Nevada Test and Training Range following aerial refuelling during Exercise Red Flag. USAF/ MSgt Kevin Gruenwald

arrive in an exercise like Red Flag to start developing game plans that involve both types. Some threats could be very susceptible to some of the Growler's jamming capabilities. Maybe we don't have to shoot weapons at those but can negate such threats by non-kinetic effects. And there may be other threats they [EA-18Gs] can't get jamming coverage on because of geometry, so we need to be ready to employ. But there are certain threats that, no matter how many HARM missiles launch, the combined effect doesn't achieve the required result to protect the striker, so we carry precision-guided munitions with which to destroy that target. It's a great mission, and I think the reason why we have so much pride in SEAD is because we support different types of aircraft by ensuring it's safe for them to get to their targets and back home."

Above: **Airmen prepare to park an F-16C Fighting Falcon for refuelling during an edition of exercise Iron Hand at North Auxiliary Airfield, South Carolina.** USAF/SrA Isaac Nicholson

said: "After gathering what we've learned from commander-led experimentation, we are now moving forward into a season of standardisation. The COMO structure allows fighter wings to prepare for rapid deployments and to disaggregate and reaggregate as needed by the CFACC [Combined Force Air Component Commander]."

The initiative is the first phase of a broader force presentation model being built by Air Combat Command to better organise, train, and equip combat air forces. Phase two will focus on evaluation of air base squadrons that can rapidly deploy and provide base operating support. Phase three examines wing command and control capabilities. The Shaw-based 20th FW and the Hill-based 388th FW and its associated 419th FW were the first wings to transition to the COMO model.

Discussing COMO, Cass said: "Each FGS has a squadron commander and an operations officer. That means I have a counterpart on the FGS that I can talk to who is typically one rank below the fighter squadron commander just because it's a new concept and the maintenance community does not have the depth yet to fill the leadership positions with higher ranking folks. But that doesn't matter. I know he's doing the best to take care of his guys and his jets and my pilots, and I'm doing my best to only request what we need to get my pilots their required training or make the maintainers work harder than they need to. It's been successful so far.

"On the final day of Checkered Flag 22-1, the 'Tigers' launched all scheduled lines [aircraft] in the morning, and then got all 16 aircraft home in the afternoon, all after a two-week exercise. That's incredible because our jets are not new. What the maintainers can do and put together, to keep them available for the flight schedule is amazing, the FGS is truly a sister squadron."

AFFORGEN

After the US Air Force introduced its Air Force Force Generation (AFFORGEN) model in August 2021, the 20th FW accelerated its force generation approach, sustained readiness, and delivered three major aviation deployments in calendar year 2022. These included back-to-back deployments to Prince Sultan Air Base (PSAB) by the 77th and 79th FSs, which demonstrated the wing's capability to supply airmen and airpower to the Joint Force.

After just 18 months from the previous CENTCOM deployment by a 20th FW squadron, the 77th Expeditionary Fighter Squadron (EFS), 77th Expeditionary Fighter Generation Squadron (EFGS), and an additional team of airmen assigned to the 20th Maintenance Squadron returned to PSAB to support operations within the US CENTCOM area of responsibility.

The 77th EFGS was responsible for the launch, recovery, and overall maintenance for every F-16 Fighting Falcon aircraft, while assigned to PSAB.

Generating a deployment for an F-16 squadron to project combat airpower across the CENTCOM theatre, is a strategic undertaking, requiring manpower and logistical support. Maintaining F-16s, and ensuring they are ready to carry out mission objectives once they've arrived in the AOR, presents other challenges that require the expertise of airmen from different specialties, including crew chiefs AND weapons load crews to ensure safe munitions loading, resulting in properly loaded munitions that are ready to be deployed, support avionics, electrical and environmental.

First time core wing

As part of its first deployment to Exercise Red Flag at Nellis since 2021, the 20th FW participated in Red Flag 23-2 for the first time as the core wing. It worked directly with all the participants daily, providing administration and mess facilities to all 1,800 personnel assigned to the 21 participating units. The 20th FW personnel also helped co-ordinate maintenance support, access equipment and materials, facility access and a variety of other tasks to get the units what they needed.

The exercise provided more complex target areas, camouflage, and concealment techniques in multiple spectrums, and introduced

Above: **A crew chief assigned to the 79th Fighter Generation Squadron prepares to marshal an F-16C Fighting Falcon at Shaw Air Force Base, South Carolina.** USAF/A1C Steven Cardo

realistic scenarios forcing re-attacks in accordance with acceptable levels of risk. The 20th FW generated and flew sorties over the course of a two-week period and gained invaluable simulated combat experience and lessons learned to take into the next real-world deployment tasking.

The 55th FGS 'Shooters' sent 130 personnel and 14 aircraft for the 17-day exercise, flew 190 sorties and more than 450 hours, and the 79th FGS deployed 128 personnel and 14 aircraft, completing 186 sorties and more than 451 hours flown.

F-16 modernisation

As part of the US Air Force's F-16 Service Life Extension Program (SLEP), maintainers assigned to the 55th, 77th and 79th FGSs worked with personnel assigned to the SLEP to install the Northrop Grumman APG-83 Scalable Agile Beam Radar, a multifunction, active electronically scanned array radar.

The F-16 SLEP is designed to extend the F-16's service life from 8,000 to 12,000 hours, and to keep the jets in service until nearly 2050. It combines a dozen structural modifications in one package – from bulkheads to wings and canopy, part of 22 modification upgrades. At Shaw, the three fighter generation squadrons fitted the APG-73 radar to more than 70 F-16s.

The APG-83 radar allows the pilot to use synthetic aperture radar mapping to detect and deploy weapons against air-to-air and air-to-ground threats at much longer ranges, keeping the aircraft in the fight. The modernisation

Left: **An F-16C Fighting Falcon assigned to the 79th Fighter Squadron takes off from Nellis Air Force Base during Exercise Red Flag.** USAF/ SSgt Madeline Herzog

work lasted into 2024 and at its completion made the 20th FW the largest combat-coded active-duty F-16 wing in the US Air Force.

Contingency breakout

During the late summer of 2023, airmen assigned to the 20th Equipment Maintenance Squadron (EMS), specialising in precision guided munitions (PGM), exercised contingency breakout procedures on live munitions at Shaw AFB.

The exercise simulated a rapid response force generation scenario in which PGM specialists unpacked, inspected, and prepared live munitions for service directly from storage to further strengthen the squadron's agile combat employment (ACE) capabilities.

Commenting on the exercise, Master Sergeant Craig Miezejeski, 20th EMS PGM non-commissioned officer in charge, said: "As we move toward an ACE environment, it's a minimal footprint procedure. The contingency breakout inspection procedures are written in a manner where we prioritise the major discrepancies that cause weapons failure and mission degradation. The procedures are then focused less on the lifespan of the missile and more on getting it into the fight as quickly as possible."

ACE: Exercise Tiger Claw

During a three-day ACE generation exercise, the 79th FS and 79th FGS conducted Tiger Claw 24-2 to simulate aircraft generation from separate forward operating locations. The objective was to help the air force develop new methods

of efficiently assembling equipment packages for deployment and better execute ACE in a contested threat environment.

The exercise tasked two teams of airmen to prepare and generate 12 combat capable aircraft from separate locations with limited time and resources, encouraging the teams to problem-solve and achieve mission success under pressure.

The exercise was unique to the 79th FS which had to determine what was required to make packages of equipment work in two separate light and lean locations and execute ACE.

Record keepers

Personnel who work in Squadron Aviation Resource Management (SARM), the record keeping for flight hours, flight operations, and pilot records, keep everything managed and organised. Flight hour programme reports help the maintenance group allocate manning and resources required to fix aircraft.

Manning, funding, and other resources are all reported by SARM personnel. They work closely with pilots to relay information from leadership to make sure they meet flight hour quotas for safety, training, and certification. The monthly data that comes from mission operations goes into a system that logs precise airtime statistics, providing Air Combat Command with the information needed to allocate funds across their area of responsibility. This ensures pilots have access to all resources

needed to deliver combat airpower anytime, anywhere.

By understanding specialty codes, SARM personnel streamline communication with the maintenance teams, enabling them to begin troubleshooting in-flight aircraft before the pilot lands. SARM reports also aid maintenance teams to proactively craft servicing plans, reduce aircraft downtime and provide more frequent training opportunities.

Getting parts

When an aircraft requires service, maintainers contact the parent wing's logistics readiness squadron materiel management flight to acquire aircraft parts to fix the problem.

At Shaw, the 20th Logistics Readiness Squadron (LRS) materiel management flight consists of various shops, including an aircraft parts store (APS) and mobility readiness spares packages (MRSP). The APS is responsible for housing daily aircraft equipment, supporting the 55th, 77th and 79th FGS, the 20th Component Maintenance Squadron (CMS), and the 20th EMS. The MRSP, however, is accountable for storing aircraft parts for future temporary duty (TDY) assignments, deployments, and other bases in need.

Receiving new equipment each month requires personnel to strategically store the parts to maximise utilisation of warehouse space, which they accomplish effectively by re-warehousing consistently. Re-warehousing entails airmen

Above: **An F-16C Fighting Falcon assigned to the 55th Fighter Squadron at Nellis Air Force Base, Nevada.** USAF/SSgt Madeline Herzog

efficiently finding better ways to organise equipment each time they receive another load of parts.

The APS provides day-to-day aircraft parts that are needed to ensure the aircraft is fully equipped and capable of taking off safely, with 24-hour coverage, including weekends and holidays, with a member on stand-by duty in case of emergencies.

Above: **An F-16D Fighting Falcon assigned to the 55th Fighter Squadron receives final checks before taxiing to the runway during Exercise Red Flag at Nellis Air Force Base.** USAF/SSgt Madeline Herzog

Left: **F-16C Fighting Falcons assigned to the 20th Fighter Wing prepare to taxi on the flight line at Nellis Air Force Base, Nevada.** USAF/SSgt Madeline Herzog

When an FGS goes on a TDY or deployment, it doesn't have access to the APS, instead, they rely on the MRSP to provide kits that contain all the necessary equipment to support and sustain flight operations from the deployed location.

Keeping things moving

Airmen and equipment are crucial to mission success and the implementation of the AFFORGEN model, so airmen who conduct logistics planning co-ordinate the swift and safe launch and retrieval of all assets.

The AFFORGEN cycle is to commit, prepare, reset, and certify, throughout, which airmen working in logistics planning play a large part in aligning the wing to meet its mission objectives. LRS personnel disseminate information to units across the wing early, ensuring tasks needed for temporary duties and deployments can be completed in advance. Airmen in their deployment cycle can be summoned at a moment's notice, so by meeting departure timelines the wing can continue its mission.

Preparation and certification go hand in hand. Exercises like Iron Hand, Ready Eagle and Bamboo Eagle allow

Above: **F-16C Fighting Falcon 93-0550/SW of the 55th Fighter Squadron, with full colour tail markings, lands at Nellis on its arrival for Exercise Red Flag.** USAF/SrA Megan Estrada

the 20th FW to practise how it will play downrange. Whether the application is a local or geographically separated exercise, making sure all essential parties are there requires copious planning. Once mandatory items are entered into the inventory, 20th LRS airmen co-ordinate with neighbouring bases to schedule deliveries, and by doing so strengthen interoperability within the force. Once the training objectives are executed, data from that training is used to build an after-action report. Successfully executing exercises keeps the wing in line with mission standards.

When the tasking requires the 20th FW to operate downrange, airmen assigned to the 20th LRS expedite the process, move to 24-hour operations to guarantee that no stone is left unturned when planning massive movements.

Safely and efficiently delivering operations at an overseas location is a priority for 20th LRS airmen and posturing for operations to return home after executing the mission is a full circle responsibility.

Logistics planning airmen now use a paperless cargo transport system that makes it easier to account for inventory, expediting the time that cargo recovery teams can verify that everything arrived intact. By expediting a process that used to take several hours to a single hour, the personnel deployment function process enables airmen to depart to execute the mission quicker.

Checkered Flag

In May 2024, the 79th FS and the 79th FGS took part in Checkered Flag 24-2 and a Weapons System Evaluation Program (WSEP) at Tyndall AFB, Florida.

Checkered Flag is a large force exercise that involves 50 or more aircraft from across the joint branches. It is designed to prepare units for immediate missions by improving air combat tactics, aerial refuelling operations, and overall mission effectiveness. Concurrently, Combat Archer, Air Combat Command's WSEP, provides aircrew with live-fire training and evaluates weapons systems and tactics in simulated combat scenarios.

WSEP provides ground crews and pilots with air-to-air missile and cannon live-fire training and focuses on evaluating and validating weapons systems and tactics in simulated combat scenarios. The exercise supplies crucial data to system engineers, allowing them to improve aircraft and munition guidance systems for the Department of Defense.

Explaining the objectives, Technical Sergeant Justin Talbert, 79th FGS weapons expeditor, said: "We fire live missiles for two reasons: to gather data on how the weapons systems will work and to give our pilots and loaders an opportunity to work with live munitions, some for the first time in their careers. Day-to-day, we train with combat arms training and maintenance missiles which have all the same technology, but don't have the warhead. This exercise gives

our people the opportunity to handle the real thing and provides much more realistic training."

During Checkered Flag, the 79th FS and the 79th FGS generated 111 sorties and flew over 230 hours.

Punching it at Iron Hand

Exercise Iron Hand is an annual week-long exercise focused on enhancing combat readiness and operational proficiency. The exercise simulates real-world scenarios, preparing airmen for a variety of potential conflicts. The 77th FS deployed four F-16s and 94 airmen to North Auxiliary Airfield for the exercise, beginning on May 13, 2025.

Describing Iron Hand, Lt Col Jordan Kahn, 20th FW chief of staff said: "These exercises support the air force's concept of agile combat employment by putting small, multi-capable teams out at forward operating sites and then further dispersing them with even smaller teams."

Throughout the exercise, participants engaged in multiple scenarios designed to test their skills and adaptability. These included rapidly regenerating combat sorties, ground attack missions, co-ordination with allied forces, and standing up the Wing Operations Center (WOC) at Shaw.

Explaining, Kahn said: "The benefits of standing up the WOC is the air force's vision for the key command and control node for the wing to support all assigned and attached forces. We liaise with higher headquarters, turning operational level planning into tactical level execution. For the units, we provide all aspects of mission planning, operations centre control, maintenance operations, logistics operations and real-time intelligence."

Iron Hand 24-3 was the first in which the 20th EMS munitions flight participated in-person. Typically, the flight builds munitions in advance to be airlifted to the location at the start of the exercise, but in Iron Hand 24-3 the flight has everything on-site, testing its effectiveness in the environment its ability to integrate with other units, furthering ACE concepts.

The flight built up 240 sticks of chaff and flare and nine bombs in the middle of the field which is not the usual way. Airmen had to deal with limited equipment, with their limited experience, but accomplish the mission. It is the perfect way to accurately size a deployed team, which core competencies are needed, and how to be agile without the full support of the main operating base.

Chromate-free primer

Between February 26 and March 11, 2025, the 20th FW's corrosion control section applied a new HS2118 primer for the first time as part of a repaint of an F-16C. The new primer was approved for field use in December 2024, replacing the chromated yellow epoxy primer previously used. Unlike its predecessor, HS2118 is non-chromated, offering a safer, environmentally friendly alternative for airmen during the painting process. It ensures proper adhesion, durability, and corrosion protection against moisture, saltwater, and temperature fluctuations, extending the aircraft's lifespan and resistance to wear and tear.

For the airmen applying the paint, HS2118 decreases their exposure to cancer-causing chemicals and reduces hazardous fumes and particulates, improving the overall work environment. According to Technical Sergeant Jeffrey Kempton, 20th EMS wing corrosion manager, the non-chromated primer still meets the corrosion inhibition and coating adhesive properties of the previous primers and will be used with non-chromated pre-treatment and topcoat.

Back to CENTCOM

In mid-April 2025, the 55th EFS deployed to the US Central Command area of responsibility, the 20th FW's latest deployment to the region. The aircraft returned to the United States in early September.

Below: Seen landing at Nellis on for Exercise Red Flag, this F-16C Fighting Falcon 91-0379/SW of the 79th Fighter Squadron is the Tigers' flagship, and features full colour tail markings. USAF/ William Lewis

GUNSLINGERS

Moody Air Force Base, Georgia has been home station to the A-10-equipped 23rd Fighter Group since 2007. The group will be the final A-10 operator in Air Combat Command.

REVERED AS AN attack aircraft, the dwindling fleet of A-10C Thunderbolt II aircraft has an average age of 42 years. Few pilots assigned to the 23rd Fighter Group (FG) and its two squadrons are older than the aircraft they fly day-to-day.

The aircraft's reverence was earned throughout the past 30 years over Afghanistan and Iraq. Ask any troop from any coalition armed service engaged in a firefight with enemy troops that received close air support (CAS) from an A-10 what their sentiments are for the aircraft, and you will receive a response full of praise for the gun-toting jet and its pilot. Many owe their lives to the A-10.

Its array of munitions ranges from the GAU-8 cannon that is capable of smothering a target with 30mm high-explosive rounds to the 2.75in laser-guided rocket for heavier fire support to the precision delivery of a 500lb GPS-guided Joint Direct Attack Munition (JDAM) often selected for a hard target.

Moody's 23rd FG has two combat-coded squadrons assigned: the 74th and 75th Fighter Squadrons operating the latest A-10C variant with a combined annual funding for upwards of 10,000 hours. The A-10C is the model modernised under the Precision Engagement Program. Colour multi-function displays, a helmet-mounted cueing system, a hands-on throttle and stick controller, digital stores management, improved fire-control, full integration of GPS-guided weapons, advanced data links, integrated sensors and a Sniper targeting pod. The A-10C entered service in 2006 and entered combat for the first time over Iraq in 2007 with the Maryland Air National Guard's 104th Fighter Squadron.

Today's A-10C fleet is configured with the Suite 11 Operational Flight Program which provides the following capabilities:

- A new High Resolution Display System (HRDS), a 11.6in HD colour primary flight display
- GBU-39 Small Diameter Bomb integration will yield a four-fold increase in standoff strike range for higher threat environments
- 3-D audio
- Jam-resistant GPS
- ARC-210 radio upgrade
- New map software
- Weapons delivery enhancement.

Below: **A-10C Thunderbolt II aircraft assigned to the 75th Expeditionary Fighter Squadron at Osan Air Base, Republic of Korea, during a routine theatre support package.** USAF/ SSgt Craig Cisek

Above: **The effectiveness of the 30mm GAU-8 Avenger rotary cannon helped the A-10 to earn the respect and gratitude of many coalition troops.** USAF/ SSgt Joe McFadden

A-10C STORES AND ARMAMENT

One internally mounted 30mm seven-barrel GAU-8/A cannon with 1,174 high-explosive incendiary/armour-piercing incendiary rounds
Up to 16,000lb of mixed ordnance on eight under-wing and three under-fuselage pylon stations
Four AIM-9 Sidewinder air-to-air missiles
AAQ-33 Sniper advanced targeting pod
AGM-65 Maverick air-to-ground missiles, including the upgraded laser-guided variant
AGR-20 2.75in rockets fitted with laser-guidance tail kits
ALQ-184 electronic countermeasure pod
CBU-87 Combined Effects Munition
CBU-89 Mine Dispensing Munition
CBU-7 Sensor Fused Weapon
CBU-100 Mk20 Rockeye II Cluster Bomb Unit
CBU-105 Wind Corrected Munitions Dispenser
GBU-12 500lb Paveway II laser-guided bomb
GBU-38 500lb Joint Direct Attack Munition
GBU-54 500lb Laser Joint Direct Attack Munition
GBU-31 2,000lb Joint Direct Attack Munition series
Mk82 500lb and Mk84 2,000lb low/high drag bombs

Training

A-10C pilot training is now conducted by the 47th Fighter Squadron, an Air Force Reserve Command unit based at Davis-Monthan Air Force Base (AFB), Arizona. Training roles include day and night weapons and tactics employment, day and night aerial refuelling, and dissimilar air combat manoeuvres. Junior pilots are trained to plan, co-ordinate, execute, and control day and night CAS and battlefield surveillance and reconnaissance. Pilots who graduate from the 47th's course are certified as combat mission ready, with their combat-mission-ready (CMR) certification.

Upon arrival at the 23rd FG, a pilot undertakes a syllabus of CMR certification training. This starts with a local orientation flight for airspace familiarisation and for them to commence flying again as there's usually a gap between the end of their course with the 47th and their arrival at Moody. They then start the CAS phase which includes a basic surface attack (BSA) mission flown to a range under degraded operational conditions, which is a slightly more of an advanced level than that provided by the 47th, in which certain systems are not working, but the pilot is still able to expend ordnance off the aircraft. Subsequent missions include a low threat scenario in the CAS environment, then in a high threat scenario, one air-to-air sortie and possibly a night-time aerial refuelling event.

This situation is caused by one or a combination of reasons: the training timeline, severe weather, or a lack of available tankers. Consequently, junior pilots might leave the 47th without completing night-time aerial refuelling.

Explaining other aspects of the upgrade training programme, former 23rd FG commander, Col Sean Baerman said: "Each new wingman will do a combat verification. An academic scenario led by a weapons officer, and which usually involves new intel personnel, new pilots and potentially a new flight lead; somebody who has recently been upgraded from wingman to flight lead. The group is given a scenario, in a specific theatre with certain threats and must plan a mission against that. It's also a more in-depth test of their general knowledge of the threats, the weapon systems in the aircraft, and their tactical knowledge of employment. Once a junior pilot completes their verification mission, they are certified as combat ready.

"Their weekly flight operations then begin during which they fly any type of mission scheduled by their squadron, not least those conducted to collaborate with other fighter units and Joint Terminal Air Controllers [JTAC] who deploy to Moody to use the local airspace and ranges. Such training allows Moody-based A-10 pilots to refine their CAS performance and cadence while working with a JTAC which is an important part of their training, and practise dissimilar air combat training with visiting fighters."

Baerman said a lot of the advanced training comes from participation in different exercises like Red Flag and maritime exercises staged by the US Navy. He said: "We support the Green Flag series of exercises, in which we provide close air support on a very large scale with the US Army on the Fort Irwin range, which is key, and the new Agile Flag exercises which meet the US Air Force's shift in focus to other threats by trending towards lead wing and ACE [agile combat employment] operations. Some of the maritime training is relevant to the threats in the Indo-Pacific theatre for maritime strike for which the A-10 has the required capabilities. We take a four-ship to support carrier operations and practise some anti-maritime ops."

Away from exercise participation, week-to-week operations at Moody include individual pilot upgrades from wingman to flight-lead to multi-ship flight-lead to instructor.

Combat search and rescue (CSAR) is another role undertaken by the A-10 and for training purposes requires complex scenarios. Outlining the processes, Baerman said: "We'll take a full-day mission plan with our HH-60W and HC-130J counterparts assigned to the 347th Rescue Group also based at Moody, and whatever ground units are available to be involved, and stage a CSAR scenario. Such missions are used to qualify our pilots for specific upgrades from Sandy 4, wingman, to Sandy 3, flight-lead, to Sandy 2, advanced flight-lead, and Sandy 1, the overall mission commander for any CSAR scenario. This type of mission requires a lot of assets and personnel, but we have a lot of success from this regular training. We have a great working relationship with the 347th Rescue Group and when we can align our assets together for full scenario training, it's very useful."

Weapon employment training

As the US Air Force's premier CAS aircraft, an A-10 goes into combat with a significant weapon payload which requires the pilot to undertake a lot of weapon employment training from the GAU-8 gun to precision-guided munitions, and occasionally a Sidewinder air-to-air missile.

Less than two miles from Moody's runway is the Grand Bay range complex. Having a local range allows A-10 pilots to shoot 30mm rounds and drop BDU-33 practice bombs during most missions. However, Grand Bay range is not used for live weapon employment. For live weapon employment, Moody's A-10 squadrons deploy to Eglin AFB, Florida, to participate in Combat Hammer, Air Combat Command's Weapon System Evaluation Program (WSEP), an evaluation of the process of assembling, loading, and dropping air-to-ground munitions.

The squadrons also undertake many temporary deployments to Nellis AFB, Nevada to participate in exercise Red Flag and to provide support to the US Air Force Weapons School course. Both events usually involve live weapon employment, as do deployments to Davis-Monthan AFB, Arizona where the squadrons participate in the Red Flag-Rescue exercise.

Baerman added that targeting pods integrated on the A-10C and its digital capability means pilots can practise dropping JDAM munitions in a synthetic way without a munition being loaded and coming off the jet.

Agile combat employment

For most US Air Force strike aircraft, operating under the ACE concept is new. For the A-10C that is not the case. During the Cold War, A-10s operated in West Germany flying off autobahns at remote locations. Because of the aircraft's unique

Below: **An A-10C Thunderbolt II assigned to the 23rd Fighter Group over the Barry M. Goldwater Range in Arizona during the Hawgsmoke gunnery competition in 2016.** USAF/A1C Mya Crosby

capabilities, such austere operations come easily to the A-10. Taking up the story, Baerman said: "We've been landing and practising off dirt strips for a long time, [and] we've been doing highway strip operations for a long time; we don't take a lot of fuel compared to some of the other fighters. Operations are pretty simple for us, and we've been used to operating from a forward location as a package, out of non-traditional airfields. So ACE is not revolutionary for us, but it is good to see that the air force is focusing some training on it because it keeps us very relevant.

"Much of what we're doing with the ACE concept isn't specific to the aircraft, it's more for airmen training. The US Air Force is trending toward a concept that whatever specialty code an airman has, they will undertake other roles. So, an ammo troop who only deals with loading missiles and munitions, will undertake another task, or a line maintainer might refuel the aeroplane as well as fix certain issues. And the 23rd FG is getting innovative with its training provision. Moody-based maintenance personnel are not only trained on the A-10, but [learn] how to service other aircraft during an ACE operation at a forward base we've set-up. To date, we've completed a couple of lead wing exercises called Mosaic Tiger when we use Moody as a main operating base, but forward deploy to Avon Park, Florida,

and other locations. The concept uses a hub and multiple spokes from where we can operate for a short amount of time before moving to another location also without set infrastructure. We are looking to expand that concept to land on other airfields perhaps using taxiways, and highways."

Thunderbolt's ops tempo

Despite the US Air Force's A-10 divestment plan, the Moody-based squadrons are operating to a significant operational tempo. Because of operations in Afghanistan and the Middle East over the past 20 years, A-10 deployment cycles were very heavy due to the nature of the aircraft's role and the support required for all coalition troops.

Commenting on the workload of the A-10 force, Baerman said: "We don't know how our ops tempo will flesh out. Our mission is to support any troops on the ground, American or coalition alike, and that mission is not going to go away. The A-10 is still the best suited fighter to do that."

Combat experiences

During his combat deployment to Afghanistan, when Baerman flew with the now disbanded Davis-Monthan-based 354th Fighter

Squadron, they initially operated from Kandahar before operations shifted to Bagram. Its primary mission was to support special operations forces and Afghan National Army troops with the latest weapon load outs that included GBU-38 and GBU-54 JDAM munitions, 2.75in rockets fitted with AGR-20 laser guidance kits and upgraded laser-guided Maverick air-to-ground missiles. Baerman described the laser-guided rocket as extremely capable in a CAS environment and confirmed the weapon was used a lot in operations.

Baerman described some examples of CAS scenarios: "The best-case scenario is when you have a complete lay down of the ground units involved, loaded in a specific electronic flight bag [tablet] that has the ground lay down and what routes you are going to take. Buildings are numbered, and you know you're going to support a specific operation, what that operation is going to entail, when it's going to start, when it's going to end, and which aeroplanes are going to replace you when you're done. Before the JTAC calls you in, he will elect the necessary weapons required: the gun, munitions, AGR-20s, or other.

"The worst-case scenario is when you get the plan for an operation and as soon as you're airborne you get re-roled to a higher priority tasking or an emerging

Below: **A-10s assigned to the 23rd Fighter Group fly in formation with a KC-135R assigned to Utah Air National Guard's 151st Air Refueling Wing during a cross-country flight From Moody to Nellis Air Force base, Nevada.** USANG/ TSgt John Winn

Above: **A-10C Thunderbolt II aircraft assigned to the 74th Fighter Squadron taxies to the runway at Moody Air Force Base, Georgia on July 11, 2017.** USAF/SrA Greg Nash

Left: **Three 23rd Fighter Group A-10C aircraft parked on the flight lines at Keesler Air Force Base, Mississippi.** USAF/A1C Kaleb Tewes

Left: **An A-10C assigned to the 74th Fighter Squadron parked on the flight line at Keesler Air Force Base, Mississippi, on August 20, 2025, during a close air support training exercise with joint terminal air controllers.** USAF/A1C Kaleb Tewes

troops-in-contact situation. It could be something as simple as supporting another operation that didn't originally have A-10s assigned and may have had other aeroplanes that either weren't able to make it or they needed more firepower, so they call us in as well. That's when you show up to the area of operation with a radio frequency to talk to somebody, and you have to deal with whatever emerges. That's CAS on the fly when you're kind of less prepared.

"There were other scenarios when we were the only aeroplanes airborne with ordnance that's needed for a high value target, such as a pop-up type or where Afghan forces are under fire. When we had multiple fighter squadrons in Afghanistan, the A-10 squadrons based at Kandahar were tasked in the southern half of the country, and the units at Bagram stuck to the northern half. Once we had less of an air presence in country, we supported all around the country."

The author asked about the challenges pilots encounter as they arrive on scene guided by the JTAC who provides the detail on the situation at hand: target ID, weapon selection, set up and strike. Baerman said: "There is always the question in the flying world as to what makes a good pilot. In my opinion a great fighter pilot is somebody who can make quick decisions in a very free flowing and dynamic environment. Our

former 75th FS commander, Lt Col Aaron Brady, always said a good CAS pilot brings order to chaos.

"Take Afghanistan where there wasn't much of a threat against us in the air depending on altitude. We were fortunate to be a little bit above the threats in Afghanistan when we were supporting troops taking direct fire. When talking with a JTAC who is trying to sort out the ground situation, we can take a god's eye view of the area to make a little bit of sense of the situation and put a little order into the chaos by precisely employing a weapon to diffuse the situation on the ground."

Baerman described how the A-10's low noise footprint was often used to advantage. He said: "That was a very common tactic in Afghanistan on both sides of the spectrum. Because the A-10 is not very loud, we were able to remain on scene outside of audible range. The insurgents couldn't hear you coming which was very effective when you wanted to employ a weapon.

"Our ability to fly low and dispense a lot of flares makes some sight, and as soon as we put an A-10 overhead a known battle, and the insurgents saw the aircraft, sometimes that in itself would break the contact because they knew how effective A-10s can be. It's both dissuasive for the enemy, but also motivational for any friendly forces on the ground."

Maintenance

Maintaining FY78 and FY79 A-10s to a mission capable standard repeatedly is no easy task. Commenting on the work undertaken by the 23rd Maintenance Group, Baerman said: "The Fighter Group's relationship with the Maintenance Group is fantastic. I think the unique challenges of working on an ageing fleet is more difficult than some of the newer aeroplanes. But the design of the A-10 is a testament to the engineers in the 70s as they built the aircraft, and it remains one of the easier aeroplanes to work on. You can swap the right and left gear, the right and left vertical stabilisers, and the engines right and left. It's a hardy aeroplane, and the

Above left: **Airmen assigned to the 23d Aircraft Maintenance Squadron, load a practise bomb onto an A-10C Thunderbolt II during Mosaic Tiger 21-1.** USAF/Airman Rachel Perkinson

Above: **Two members of a load crew fasten a practise bomb onto an A-10C Thunderbolt II during Mosaic Tiger 21-1.** USAF/Airman Rachel Perkinson

Left: **A member of the 74th Aircraft Maintenance Unit weapons load crew chief waits to load a BDU-50 practice bomb onto an A-10C Thunderbolt II during an integrated combat turn at Moody Air Force Base as part of Mosaic Tiger 21-1.** USAF/Airman Rachel Perkinson

maintainers face unique challenges with the ageing fleet, but they do a fantastic job in the current situation."

Flying the A-10

Asked what the A-10 is like to fly, Baerman commented that anyone who knows the A-10 wishes they could fly it. "It flies like a traditional aeroplane," he said. "The stick is in your lap, you have full motion versus a side stick as per the F-16, and its straight wings make it very manoeuvrable. You point the pipper on the target, and the gun was as accurate as it can be.

"Because it doesn't have such a wide turning radius, when you can come off target, you can immediately turn and roll back in within 30 seconds. That keeps enemy heads down, and if you're firing at them, they're not firing at your friendlies. With an A-10 in such a scenario putting rounds down every 15 seconds is very effective."

Fighter Generation Squadrons

On January 14, 2022, the 23rd Aircraft Maintenance Squadron (AMS) deactivated and the 74th and 75th Fighter Generation Squadrons (FGS) were activated at Moody AFB. A significant event for the 23rd FG.

The new structure, titled Combat Oriented Maintenance Organization (COMO) levelled the maintenance organisational structure and transitioned aircraft maintenance units into fighter generation squadrons. A fighter generation squadron is a squadron composed of maintainers responsible for airpower well-being and production. The squadron will be paired with a complementary fighter squadron, and the two units will work together to ensure their squadron's aircraft are ready to fly.

The changes were implemented to develop the two new squadrons in a way that achieved not only their mission, but the mission of a Lead Wing while emulating the distinction of the former 23rd AMS.

Air-launched decoys

The 23rd Wing issued a release in March 2024 stating that airmen assigned to the 23rd Maintenance Group were training on the ADM-160 Miniature Air-Launched Decoy (MALD), a store designed to mimic other aircraft, diverting enemy fire away from pilots.

Above: **Airmen assigned to the 23d Wing prepare to refuel an A-10C Thunderbolt II using the STARCART during Mosaic Tiger 21-1.** USAF/ A1C Jasmine Barnes

Below: **The STARCART refuelling platform sits on the hot cargo pad at Moody.** USAF/Airman Rachel Perkinson

When MALDs are launched they deceive defence systems and enemy cruise missiles by giving the illusion the decoy is an aircraft. MALDs can mimic the signal of various aircraft such as B-52s, F-16s, and F-35s.

Long-time flagship

Just about all air force squadrons operate an aircraft known as a flagship. A squadron's flagship carries the squadron commander's name below the cockpit and the tail flash is painted differently to the rest of the squadron's aircraft.

One example of a flag ship was A-10C tail number 78-0674 which the 23rd Wing received on August 14, 1992, from the 354th Fighter Wing, a now disbanded wing based at the former Myrtle Beach AFB, South Carolina. Aircraft 674 was assigned to the 75th FS, at the time

the aircraft's eventual squadron, the 74th FS had not activated at Pope AFB, North Carolina, then home station of the 23rd Wing. That event took place on June 15, 1993, when the 74th was equipped with F-16Cs but subsequently started its transition to A-10As in July 1996. During the transition, aircraft 78-0674 moved over to the 74th FS and became the commander's flagship.

Between 1996 and February 27, 2024, 78-0674 was the flagship for ten 74th FS commanders, deployed six times and left Moody with 16,311.5 hours.

Load competition

Airmen from the 74th and 75th FGS compete in a quarterly load competition at Moody AFB. For three months prior to the event, the top three out of 60 weapons airmen are chosen to compete at the load competition held in front of an audience of co-workers, leadership, and family members.

Describing the competition, Chief Master Sergeant William Beard, 23rd Maintenance Group weapons manager, said: "Load crew of the quarter events are conducted throughout the year to highlight the best and the brightest, most proficient weapons load crews from both fighter generation squadrons. We see who can load the weapons the fastest, without any safety or liability violations."

Meticulous attention to detail and standards is paramount, especially when dealing with potentially deadly ammunition in austere conditions when

Below: **The shark teeth nose art applied to an A-10C assigned to the 23rd Fighter Group.** USAF/ A1C Kaleb Tewes

deployed overseas, so weapons loading is one of four scored parts of the event.

Explaining the scoring, Beard said: "We test them on weapons, munitions systems and aircraft knowledge. We look over their uniforms, haircuts, boots, patches, toolboxes are inspected for cleanliness and organisation. It's a two-week effort to make sure all those things are aligned and prepared for, culminating in the final load."

With tightened timelines, spectators and peer pressure, the airman must look over the missile launchers, bomb racks and the munition itself before they can begin to load, secure the munition to

the aircraft, and get ready for flight – all while following a series of checklists and technical orders to ensure accuracy and safety.

Shark teeth

Following the 23rd Wing's Flying Tigers heritage from World War Two when its aircraft carried shark teeth markings, the 23rd FG's A-10s carry similar markings. Airmen assigned to the 23rd Maintenance Squadron apply the shark teeth to each A-10 assigned to the group as part of a repaint.

Discussing a repaint, Technical Sergeant Mark King, 23rd Maintenance Squadron corrosion manager, said: "We're the only ones in the air force that apply the shark teeth and it means a lot to be able to represent it."

Repainting is part of routine jet maintenance – whenever an aircraft returns to Moody from a maintenance depot with new paint, it needs to be finished with the markings, tail flashes and the famous shark teeth nose art, requiring a multi-step week-long process.

Detailing the repainting process, Staff Sergeant William Rogers, a structural maintenance craftsman assigned to the 23rd Maintenance Squadron, said:

"First and foremost, before the aircraft even rolls into the paint barn, it will be washed. The next steps are sanding everything off that is not going to get painted. After that, we mask and re-mask the jet – putting it through the multiple colours, stencils, and different curing times."

Equipped with a specialised jet-sized paint booth, a large cutting-edge printer that can make decals and stencils, and lots of painting and protective equipment, airmen work as high-tech artists over the course of the A-10's transformation into a world-famous Flying Tiger aircraft.

Above: **The pilots of two A-10s assigned to the 74th Fighter Squadron launch flares in the skies of southern Georgia.** USAF/ SSgt Jamal Sutter

SNOOPY BIRDS

Offutt Air Force Base, near the city of Omaha in Nebraska, is home to the 55th Wing and its fleet of resplendent RC-135 reconnaissance aircraft.

N JULY, THE 55th Wing deployed RC-135 Rivet Joint aircraft to Australia for Exercise Talon Shield, part of Australia's larger exercise, Talisman Sabre. The Offutt-based wing conducted the deployment in accordance with the Air Force Force Generation model, dubbed AFFORGEN, which is designed to provide a mission-ready, sustainable component to the joint force. Airmen and the RC-135s deployed to Royal Australian Air Force (RAAF) Base Edinburgh, Australia, under the Deployable Combat Wing construct which involves small teams operating from distributed locations.

The RC-135s were joined by teams from the RQ-4 Global Hawk-equipped 319th Reconnaissance Wing based at Grand Forks AFB, North Dakota, and the E-3G-equipped 552nd Air Control Wing based at Tinker AFB, Oklahoma. Combined, the three wings provided intelligence, surveillance and reconnaissance, airborne command and control, and electromagnetic warfare capabilities.

Standing up a Deployable Combat Wing in Australia required meticulous planning, cross-unit synchronisation and a logistics effort between

the Nebraska, North Dakota, and Oklahoma-based wings.

For the Offutt-based 55th Wing, participating in Talon Shield involved deploying nearly 200 personnel including aircraft maintenance, operations, intelligence, communications, security forces, logistics and personnel support, and 55 tons of cargo including mission-critical systems, maintenance equipment, aircraft support tools, communications infrastructure, and supplies. Moving so many people, aircraft and equipment required collaboration between US Transportation Command based at Scott AFB, Illinois, Pacific Air Forces based at Hickam AFB, Hawaii, and the RAAF.

Explaining the logistics involved, Col Alfred Rosales said: "The logistical operation spanned hemispheres. Our ability to seamlessly arrive, set-up and operate with the RAAF shows what allied nation integration looks like in action. It's not theory, it's a capability realised."

The operation was also required a combat-ready team, fully integrated and postured to execute the mission from day one. Every element from aircraft and equipment to fuel plans and lodging was in place to ensure airmen could arrive, plug in, and immediately contribute to the fight, an example of the successful implementation of the AFFORGEN model.

Outlining the success of the Australian deployment, Col Aaron Gray, commander of the 55th Wing

Below: **Airmen with the 763rd Expeditionary Aircraft Maintenance Unit, prepare to place chocks for an RC-135 Rivet Joint at Al Udeid Air Base, Qatar.** USAF/TSgt Amy Lovgren

10 Squadron, and supported by 24 Squadron, Edinburgh's operations and support unit.

Out of Omaha

The 55th Wing is the host unit at Offutt AFB, Nebraska. Known as the Fighting 55th, the wing is tasked to provide information warfare forces through a range of operations. For example, electromagnetic spectrum, information, intelligence, surveillance, reconnaissance, and nuclear command, control, and communications. The primary customers for the intelligence gathered by aircraft assigned to the 55th Wing is the joint force and America's national leadership, anytime, anywhere.

Above: **An RC-135 Rivet Joint uploads fuel from a KC-135 during Exercise Talisman Sabre 25 in Northern Territory, Australia, on July 17, 2025.** USANG/SSgt Jocelyn Tuller

said: "Our team was laser focused on demonstrating both the Deployed Combat Wing concept and the importance of RC-135 Rivet Joint integration into long-range kill chain operations. With the help of our great Australian allies, we accomplished it all."

The 55th Wing completed 22-hour RC-135 Rivet Joint sorties, conducted distributed command and control operations through ground-based and airborne nodes, and operated with airmen assigned to the 319th Reconnaissance and 552nd Air Control Wing on missions involving RAAF F/A-18F Super Hornets, F-35A Lightnings and E-7A Wedgetail to execute joint targeting and kill chain processes.

The 55th Wing's deployment tested and validated the deployable combat wing concept under pressurised scenarios and exceeded the readiness metrics set by Air Combat Command, and consequently confirmed the 55th Wing's ability to generate, employ, and sustain combat power in contested, degraded, and coalition-integrated environments.

While deployed to RAAF Base Edinburgh, the 55th Wing was hosted by the RAAF's MC-55-equipped

The wing operates from multiple locations around the globe (see table). The backbone of the 55th Wing's fleet are three variants of the RC-135 with the names Cobra Ball, Combat Sent and Rivet Joint.

RC-135S Cobra Ball

ACC's 55th Wing operates three RC-135S Cobra Ball TELemetry INTelligence (TELINT) aircraft.

Cobra Ball's unique mission was originally used to monitor Soviet missile activity during the Cold War. In the post-Cold War world Cobra Ball continues to be tasked by the Joint Chiefs of Staff in the TELINT role to collect optical and electronic data from tracking ballistic

NOTABLE RIVET JOINT EVENTS

Flying at the invitation of the Finnish Defense Forces, on March 23, 2024, a US Air Force RC-135 flew a mission over Finland for the first time. The mission was flown to demonstrate US European Command's shared commitment to enhancing readiness and providing training opportunities to improve interoperability with Finland.

The 55th Operations Group Detachment 1 was activated at Elmendorf AFB on January 17, 2024. Explaining the detachment's mission at Joint Base Elmendorf-Richardson (JBER), Col Derek Rachel, 55th Operations Group commander said: "The [detachment] will be able to support the various 55th Wing missions and all our aircraft types supporting multiple combatant commands simultaneously out of JBER. Our aircraft and aircrew will operate secretary-of-defense-directed missions out of JBER or using it as a stopover point for high-priority missions to other destinations around the world."

Between August 18 and 23, 2023, Naval Support Activity (NSA) Souda Bay, Greece, provided operational and logistical support to the crew of a US Air Force RC-135 Rivet Joint assigned to the 763rd Expeditionary Reconnaissance Squadron.

The aircraft and crew were deployed to Souda Bay from Al Udeid Air Base, Qatar, to exercise the ability to generate combat missions in various locations in and out of US Central Command's area of responsibility during Operation Agile Spartan.

During 34 years of constant deployment throughout the Middle East, Rivet Joint aircraft have conducted 13,460 non-stop combat missions and completed over 145,000 flying hours in support of Operations Desert Shield, Desert Storm, Northern Watch, Southern Watch, Enduring Freedom, Iraqi Freedom, Inherent Resolve, and Spartan Shield.

Below: **Airmen with the 55th Maintenance Squadron marshal an RC-135 Rivet Joint during Red Flag 25-1 at Nellis Air Force Base, Nevada, on January 30, 2025.** USAF /TSgt Chris Thornbury

missile systems and re-entry vehicles for treaty verification in what are termed 'rest-of-world activities', China, India, and Pakistan for example. Cobra Ball is also tasked with spotting battlefield missiles, in the so-called theatre missile defence role.

A Cobra Ball flight crew consists of a minimum of two pilots and one navigator; the mission crew comprises three electronic warfare officers, two airborne systems engineers, and two or more airborne mission specialists, many of whom are also qualified for the Rivet Joint and Combat Sent missions (see later).

Each RC-135S is configured with a thimble nose, cheek fairings housing electronic receivers, and an aft fuselage teardrop-shaped antenna fairing. The RC-135S nose houses an enhanced weather radar which is used to provide very accurate positional data to the crew, which ensures that during TELINT missions, the crew stay within international airspace. The Cobra Ball radar has a tracking capability, which is used to detect missiles, cruise missiles or aircraft in the theatre missile defence role. The radar tracks the target and provides positional data in a

three-dimensional mode in all weather conditions.

The most notable modifications on a RC-135S are a row of three rectangular windows in the forward fuselage. These facilitate telescopic monitoring devices, advanced optics and infrared telescopes and sensors used for tracking ballistic missiles at long range.

The two original Cobra Ball aircraft, serial numbers 61-2662 and 61-2663, are equipped with the full SIGnals

INTelligence (SIGINT) and Measurement And Signatures INTelligence (MASINT) sensor suites to gather intelligence data from the entire electromagnetic spectrum, especially signatures and tracks associated with missiles during their boost and re-entry phases. Two sided electro-optical/infrared radiometric sensors, infrared telescopes, and spectral sensors called the Real Time Optical System (RTOS) and the Large Aperture Tracker

Right: **A crew chief opens a panel on an RC-135 Rivet Joint to check the hydraulic fluids were within operational specification and fully functional for an upcoming flight.**
USAF/TSgt Chris Thornbury

Below: **Airmen from the 55th Maintenance Squadron hook-up an air conditioning unit to an RC-135 Rivet Joint before Red Flag 25-1 at Nellis Air Force Base, Nevada on January 26, 2025. The onboard computers require a cool state to operate optimally.**
USAF/TSgt Chris Thornbury

Left: **Airmen assigned to the 343rd Reconnaissance Squadron and 97th Intelligence Squadron work with Royal Air Force crew on an RC-135 Rivet Joint during Red Flag 25-1 at Nellis Air Force Base, Nevada.** USAF/TSgt Chris Thornbury

Below: **A crew chief inspects an RC-135 Rivet Joint before flight during Red Flag 25-1 at Nellis Air Force Base, Nevada on January 28, 2025.** USAF/TSgt Chris Thornbury

A third RC-135S, 62-4128, entered service with the 45th RS in 1998 and is referred to as Cobra Ball II.

RC-135U Combat Sent

The 55th Wing also operates two RC-135U Combat Sent aircraft each configured with a short nose radome, and fairings in the chin, wingtips, tail cone and fin-top which house the Precision Power Measurement System sensors, with a 360° coverage.

The primary mission objective for Combat Sent is to locate and identify foreign military land, naval, and airborne ELectronic INTelligence (ELINT) data, deemed to be the most interesting, the so-called scientific and technical ELINT. To enable the crew to detect and filter out the most interesting ELINT data, several systems are fitted, which are believed to be unique to the RC-135U. These include a radar frequency measurement system, a spectrography and radiometer system and thermal imaging. An extensive database holds all known emitter information, which allows non-interesting signals to be eliminated quickly.

Combat Sent aircraft are believed to be fitted with the expert mission manager (EMM), an automated system that provides fast ELINT collection of short transmission and hard-to-collect signals emitted from supposedly secure communication systems. EMM operates in real-time validating and re-identifying

System (LATS) form the MASINT sensor suite.

The RTOS is a long-range sensor system, which can acquire, track and record targets in the visible and infrared spectrums. The RTOS staring sensors centred off the wings provide a target acquisition capability with a 120° arc on both sides of the aircraft. LATS is an optical telescope, which captures long-range targets in fine-resolution imagery with its 12in focal length.

Cobra Ball is also equipped with the Medium-wave InfraRed Array (MIRA) optical surveillance sensor (camera) system. MIRA cameras, fitted on both sides of the aircraft, capture missile re-entry imagery within the medium wave infrared spectrum. The MIRA system provides Cobra Ball with an advanced scientific and technical intelligence collection capability used for foreign ballistic missile system analysis and treaty verification.

Above: **A crew chief assigned to the 55th Maintenance Squadron attaches a fuel line to an RC-135 Rivet Joint post-flight during Red Flag 25-1 at Nellis Air Force Base, Nevada on January 28, 2025.** USAF/TSgt Chris Thornbury

ELINT signals against several collected ELINT signal databases.

The EMM prioritises action against signals based on location, identifies the best location for the RC-135 to collect the signal, and recommends the systems to tune for the signal collection, ensuring that unknown signals are properly recorded for analysis. The objective is to automatically process all known and usual signals away from the onboard intelligence officers, allowing them to concentrate on unknown and difficult signals.

RC-135 Rivet Joint

The US Air Force Rivet Joint fleet comprises eight RC-135Vs (originally built as C-135Bs) and nine RC-135Ws, former RC-135B aircraft. The entire conversion programme was undertaken to enable all aircraft to undertake a joint SIGINT mission, which is where the Rivet Joint name is partly derived from.

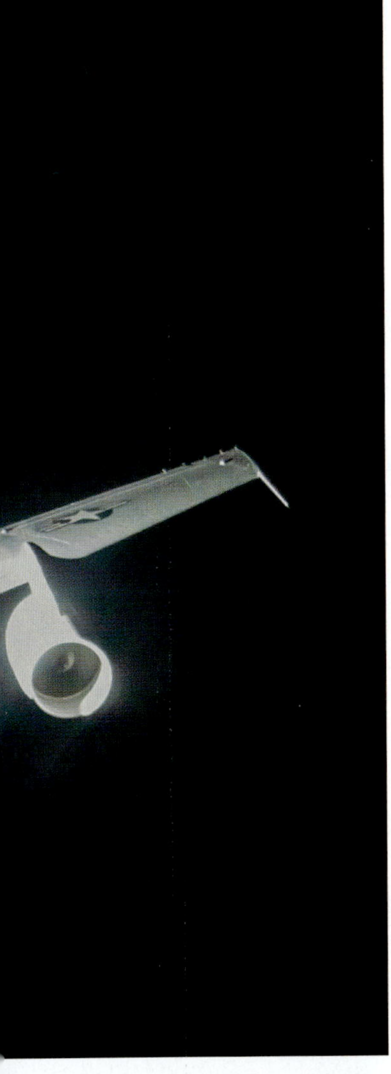

Above:
Maintaining airframes as old as the RC-135 can present real challenges to its maintainers and engineers, even without the plethora of mission systems.
US Air Force

Left: **An RC-135 Rivet Joint parked on the flightline at Nellis Air Force Base, Nevada.**
USAF/TSgt Chris Thornbury

Rivet Joint aircraft provide near real-time ELINT and communications intelligence (COMINT) collection, analysis and dissemination capabilities to US theatre and national chain of command authorities. Providing theatre commanders with ELINT and COMINT data, and specifically imminent threat and time-sensitive information about the location and intent of enemy forces.

A Rivet Joint aircraft is divided into three compartments: the flight deck populated by the pilot, co-pilot, and navigator; the RAVEN compartment which is the forward reconnaissance section used for the ELINT mission; and the operators' compartment which is the aft reconnaissance section used for the COMINT mission.

RAVENS are Electronic Warfare officers who operate the AEELS (Automatic ELINT Emitter Locator System) suite and the manually operated direction-finding antenna. The RAVEN compartment has three consoles designated RAVEN 1, 2 and 3.

RAVEN 1 hosts the tactical co-ordinator and runs the AEELS automatic collection system. RAVEN 2 (the mid console) hosts the tactical co-ordinator – the orchestrator for both the ELINT and COMINT operators. RAVEN 3 (the forward console) runs the manual collection system.

Behind the RAVEN's consoles, the most forward two operator stations are used by Airborne System Engineers (ASEs) who monitor and troubleshoot all the mission systems and undertake light maintenance. One ASE is dedicated to the ELINT systems and the other to the COMINT systems.

Positioned aft of the ASEs, are consoles used by each of the 12-person cryptologic crew comprising four management positions (one each for the data link operator, the airborne analyst, the airborne mission supervisor, and the information integration officer), and eight operator positions for cryptologic language analysts, all of whom are linguists.

Two positions further aft host a signals search and development operator, and a reconnaissance, surveillance, target acquisition operator.

RC-135 Rivet Joint cheek fairings house some of the primary ELINT side-facing antennas integrated with the AEELS, the primary system used to gather signals from across the entire electromagnetic spectrum, process them, and filter out the most significant and interesting. Selected signals are then served to the onboard operator stations for analysis by the system operators. Mission data is recorded on computer hard drives. A laser jet printer is carried to provide a hard copy printout of the collated ELINT and COMINT data.

In 1976, the first Rivet Joint aircraft, RC-135V 64-14848, was fitted with the fully automated MUltiple position COMINT Emitter Location System (MUCELS), which is a standard system throughout the fleet used to collect communication intelligence across a wide frequency band. The most visible component of the MUCELS system is the antenna farm of large plate aerials, on the fuselage underside. All Rivet Joint aircraft have satellite communication links, which are facilitated by T-shaped aerials fitted on the top of the fuselage.

Baseline upgrades

To exploit the rapid evolution of both commercial off-the-shelf and bespoke technologies, the US Air Force 645th Aeronautical Systems Group, known as the Big Safari programme office, uses an agile incremental baseline (BL) upgrade acquisition strategy to introduce new equipment and capabilities to all RC-135 series aircraft.

The US Air Force's Manned Reconnaissance Systems programme includes 17 RC-135V/W Rivet Joint, three RC-135S Cobra Ball, and two RC-135U Combat Sent mission aircraft performing Air Combat Command operational missions.

The RC-135V/W Rivet Joint is the majority variant that drives the baseline integration and modification upgrade strategy for the entire RC-135 fleet. Therefore, a significant amount of the modification budget is directly related to Rivet Joint weapon system baseline strategy enhancements which subsequently transfer into the follow-on baseline strategy enhancements for the Cobra Ball and Combat Sent weapon systems.

RC-135 viability assessments in 2008, 2012, and 2019, reported that despite the fleet average airframe age (57 years) and accumulated flight hours (42,740) as of the end of FY2018, the RC-135

Below: **An RC-135 Rivet Joint takes-off for a Weapons School Integration (WSINT) mission at Nellis Air Force Base, Nevada.** USAF/ William Lewis

would be able to continue to meet the user's needs by performing intended operations through at least 2050.

Viability was assessed based on underlying analyses of reliability, maintainability, performance, corrosion, fatigue, architectural stability, safety, and availability. The viability assessment also summarised that the RC-135 fleet has experienced significant improvements in reliability, maintainability, and availability since FY2001.

The Rivet Joint Baseline (BL) integration efforts of BL-12 and BL-13 which started in early FY2019, address the 2012 RC-135 Multi-Attribute Utility Assessment (MUA) that detailed operational effectiveness, cost, and programme analyses of the alternative weapon system configurations. The MUA determined that retaining and sustaining the RC-135V/W airframe offered the highest assessed weapons system utility (measured as a benefit of cost-to-risk ratio) over the 25-year assessment period.

BL-12 enhancements include increased digital signal exploitation, increased digital signal recorder bandwidth, enhanced spatial processing/exploitation, an enhanced weather radar, digitally enhanced electronic flight instrument system (EFIS), ongoing CNS/ATM compliant cockpit avionics enhancements, Air Force Distributed Common Ground System (AF-DCGS, see below) interoperability, operator work station 3-D map projection, enhanced operator reporting management tools, modernised communications security (COMSEC) protocols, and a new steerable beam antenna.

FY2025 procurement funding will concentrate on three major efforts: initiate the integration and testing of BL-15, continue the conversion of BL-12 aircraft into BL-14 aircraft, and continue the autopilot upgrade.

Ten Rivet Joint aircraft are projected to receive the BL-14 configuration. During this same period, Combat Sent will complete the conversion of the BL-5 aircraft to BL-6, and the Cobra Ball will continue integration and testing of the BL-14 standard.

Combat Sent and Cobra Ball baselines closely align with Rivet Joint BL-14. Additionally, FY2025 procurement will ensure integration and fielding updates to the RC-135 ground systems, which include Rivet Joint Ground Data Processing Systems (GDPS), Distributed Mission Shelters (DMS), Mission Crew Training Systems (MCTS), Airborne Capabilities Extension System (ACES), and Operational Flight Trainers (OFT).

The ground systems are upgraded to remain consistent with the fielded aircraft configurations to allow for training and qualification of the aircrew and maintenance personnel assigned, plus verification and certification of software builds that are continuously modified to address the dynamic mission requirements of these weapons systems.

Above: **An RC-135 Rivet Joint assigned to the 82nd Expeditionary Reconnaissance Squadron takes off at Kadena Air Base, Japan.** USAF/SSgt Benjamin Sutton

Enhancements focus on improving the ability of the RC-135 family of aircraft to compete and deter in the near-peer environment across the range of military operations. Due to the rapidly changing global threat environment, the acquisition programme manager has the authority to redirect funding as necessary to meet current stated and emerging combatant command and intelligence community requirements.

The Capability Description Document (CDD) addresses airframe, sensor, navigation, communications, data link, and processing requirements necessary to keep the RC-135 fleet viable through until 2050.

A Program Management Directive (PMD) provides direction to the 645th Aeronautical Systems Group (645 AESG) for the acquisition and sustainment of the weapons system, associated mission support equipment, and processing, exploitation, and dissemination tools

The 645 AESG baseline upgrade strategy requires purchase agreements for long-lead items that take approximately ten to 12 months from contract award to delivery. Items required for integration in a given baseline upgrade are contracted for purchase in the first year of the procurement funding cycle and are acquired and installed in the subsequent year. This acquisition strategy has been successful in maintaining critical combat capability in the intelligence, surveillance, and reconnaissance arena over the last 50 years.

RC-135S Cobra Ball

FY2025 procurement funding efforts will concentrate on integration and testing of Cobra Ball BL-14 enhancements and long lead items for BL-15. The BL-14 subsystem upgrades consist of but are not limited to: Foreign Instrumentation Signals Intelligence (FISINT) Direction Finding antenna; high-gain steerable-beam K-band collection antenna; Digital Data Recording, Digital Search, enhanced signal identification and classification;

CURRENT COMBAT-CODED RC-135 SQUADRONS

Squadron	Wing	Base	Major Command
38th RS Rivet Joint	55th Wing	Offutt AFB, Nebraska	ACC
45th RS Cobra Ball Combat Sent	55th Wing	Offutt AFB, Nebraska	ACC
82nd RS Rivet Joint	55th Wing	Kadena AB, Okinawa	ACC
95th RS Rivet Joint	55th Wing	RAF Mildenhall, England	ACC
343rd RS Rivet Joint	55th Wing	Offutt AFB, Nebraska	ACC

Left: **An RC-135 Rivet Joint assigned to the 763rd Expeditionary Reconnaissance Squadron takes off from Al Udeid Air Base, Qatar.** USAF/TSgt Amy Lovgren

Left: **Airmen assigned to the 21st Expeditionary Reconnaissance Squadron conduct a pre-flight inspection on an RC-135 at Naval Support Activity Souda Bay.** US Navy/Joel Diller

Middle: **Airmen assigned to the 55th Aircraft Maintenance Squadron stow an air hose from an air cart after starting an RC-135U Combat Sent's four CFM International F108-CF-201 engines at Offutt Air Force Base, Nebraska.** USAF/Lt Drew Nystrom

Below: **Crewmembers board an RC-135 Rivet Joint. The mission crew can forward gather information in a variety of formats for a wide range of consumers via the aircraft's extensive communications suite.** USAF/Lt Drew Nystrom

Target Discrimination via SATCOM, and the integration of the Rivet Joint BL-14 COMINT suite.

Funding provides logistical support efforts for the BL-14 configuration upgrades and enhancements on the three RC-135S Cobra Ball aircraft, their sensor systems, and associated ground support systems.

RC-135V/W Rivet Joint

FY2025 procurement funding will upgrade fielded Rivet Joint BL-13 configured aircraft but will concentrate on fielding BL-14 aircraft.

BL-13 enhancements include a continuous recording capability, new receivers, further CNS/ATM avionics

Above: **A RC-135 Rivet Joint, assigned to the 763rd Expeditionary Reconnaissance Squadron, flies over Afghanistan in support of Operation Enduring Freedom.** USAF

upgrades, and an advanced extremely high frequency communications suite.

Rivet Joint BL-14 upgrades consist of, but are not limited to: providing a continuous recording capability, scalable processor improvements, high probability of intercept (HPOI) receiver, Corvus Digital Receiver (CDR), Communications, Navigation, and Surveillance – Air Traffic Management (CNS-ATM) avionics upgrades such as new autopilot, automated data system-broadcast (ADS-B), and Mode 5 identify friendly or foe (IFF) systems.

Rivet Joint BL-15 upgrades consist of, but are not limited to: scalable processor improvements, Wideband Agile Receiver and Pulse Detector (WARPD), Expanded Steered Beam capability, and augmented Remote Maintenance. Funding in FY2025 through FY2029 was increased due to changes in inflation rates.

RC-135U Combat Sent

FY2025 procurement funding efforts will concentrate on supporting the fielded Combat Sent BL-6 aircraft. The BL-6 subsystem upgrades consist of, but are not limited to: Wideband collection, Scientific and Technical Processors, improved antennas, improved operator interface and reporting tools, sensor calibration/testing systems, integration of the Rivet Joint BL-13 COMINT suite, and enhancing capabilities in dense signal environments.

Initial BL-7 RF engineering and design efforts which began in FY2023 continued into FY2025 following which the programme will initiate procurement on long lead BL-7 requirements.

The GSQ-272 AF-DCGS is used by the Combat Air Force for planning and direction, collection, processing and exploitation, analysis and production, and dissemination of data from Airborne Intelligence, Surveillance and Reconnaissance (ISR) missions.

Ongoing Duty

The Rivet Joint continues to provide the backbone of the US Air Force's stand-off, medium-altitude, intelligence-gathering capability. Now that the US Navy's EP-3E ARIES II reconnaissance aircraft have been retired, Rivet Joint is the only dedicated, manned airborne SIGINT platform and MASINT collection system in the US inventory. RC-135 aircraft have supported every US operation since the end of the Cold War and have been flying daily missions in the European theatre related to the war in Ukraine.

As it stands, no replacement for the RC-135 aircraft, nor for the capabilities it offers, is in sight. Current planning envisages keeping the RC-135 in service until 2050.

Logistics and readiness

A component of the 55th Wing, the 55th Logistics Readiness Squadron (LRS) ensures personnel, equipment, and supplies are always ready to support global Air Force missions. It's the third smallest LRS in Air Combat Command but supports the second largest wing in the Air Force. Lt Col Caitlin Oviatt, 55th LRS commander, said: "Our mantra is to do hard things, and be savage, not average."

Overseeing deployment operations and managing the flow of personnel

Left: **An RC-135 Rivet Joint, assigned to the 763rd Expeditionary Reconnaissance Squadron, takes on fuel from a KC-135 Stratotanker over Afghanistan.** USAF

Above: **Linguists operating as cryptologic language analysts onboard an RC-135 Rivet Joint.** USAF

and equipment through the Offutt deployment readiness cell or issuing individual protective equipment and mobility gear for deployers, getting the job done is the focus of the 55th LRS. The squadron also manages ground transportation for on-base cargo, the air terminal function which manages aircraft cargo, petroleum, oil, and lubricants to ensure aircraft are adequately serviced and fuelled, and management of Offutt's vehicle fleet which includes snow removal equipment used by the 55th Civil Engineer Squadron.

Commenting on the output of the LRS, Master Sergeant Aaron Gonzales, 55th LRS material management superintendent said: "We might be a small LRS as far as people are concerned, but we are the most deployed and we have the most opportunity to execute. It's a broad organisation as far as what we do. We're not just focused on one thing. We are focused on the entire base organisation helping the wing be lethal and effective in executing the mission."

Red Flag and Bamboo Eagle

Between January 27 and February 14, 2025, two RC-135 Rivet Joint aircrews, a maintenance team, and a logistic readiness crew deployed to Nellis AFB, and flew with RAF 51 Squadron aircrew to undertake intelligence, surveillance, and reconnaissance missions throughout Exercises Red Flag 25-1 and Bamboo Eagle. Each crew consisted of roughly 30 personnel including pilots, navigators, electronic warfare officers, airborne cryptologic language analysts, aircraft systems engineers, and intelligence operators.

The coalition aircrews operated 11 missions, which provided critical information for leaders to make the best-informed decisions that affected the results of this large-scale exercise. They provided real-time threat information to other airborne platforms participating in high-risk scenarios.

Explaining, Technical Sergeant Thomas Astle, an airborne cryptologic language analyst with the 97th Intelligence Squadron said: "We glean the intel that we are gathering and push it out to all the players that need it. We make sure the command-and-control element and the fighters know exactly what is going on in the battlefield and what threats they are facing."

Discussing the learning process at Red Flag, Senior Airman Selina Flynn, an airborne systems engineer assigned to the 343rd Reconnaissance Squadron (RS) said: "With the rinse and repeat of Red Flag, it is a great opportunity for us to take lessons learned from the first week and apply it in the second week. We tested new tactics, techniques, and procedures for Bamboo Eagle, which provides a great environment for that."

During Bamboo Eagle, Rivet Joint aircrews practised their abilities to take proactive and reactive schemes of manoeuvres within threat timelines to increase survivability and combat power while exercising agile combat employment.

Aligned to the agile combat employment (ACE) concept of

Right: **Airborne system engineers, one dedicated to the ELINT systems and the other to the COMINT systems, monitor and troubleshoot all Rivet Joint mission systems and undertake light maintenance.** USAF

operations, on one mission the crew landed at March Air Reserve Base, California, to refuel on the ground without their maintenance personnel. They tested and demonstrated the aircrew filling non-standard roles that enable resilient and flexible logistics in support of agile combat employment to increase force survivability. The aircrew then took off from March to execute the mission at an extended duration and range.

Nebraska Air National Guard

On February 2, 2025, Nebraska Air National Guard's 170th Group, based at Offutt AFB, launched its first sorties on a drill weekend since the 238th Combat Training Squadron was redesignated as the Reconnaissance Squadron on October 18, 2024. The flight was staffed with mostly guard members, a situation resulting from the 238th's new dual mission requirement.

Personnel assigned to the 238th RS, included pilots, electronic warfare officers, and at least one of each airborne system engineer position. The 170th Maintenance Support Squadron provided eight maintainers to prepare and safely launch the jet and five maintainers to recover the jet at the end of the day.

According to Col Wendy Squarcia, 170th Group Commander: "The 170th Operations Support Squadron [OSS] provided support with weather, aircrew flight equipment, aviation resource management and airfield operations. The entire 170th Group will come together to reach our goal of weekend operations conducted by the 170th Group independently of the active duty 55th Wing."

Before flying, each member works through phase one by training with ground trainers which enable operators to simulate airborne operations. Phase two started on the Sunday when the 170th Group was able to operate a sortie, and phase three will take place only when the 170th Group is deemed ready to conduct a mission as a fully manned, trained, and deployable unit.

Outlining the next step in operating missions, Lt Col Brian Ross, 238th RS director of operations, said: "We plan to expand our next effort to include our Air Reserve Component teammates at the 49th Intelligence Squadron. This will hopefully be just the beginning of a regular effort during drill weekends to support and train our Total Force members with flying."

Commenting on the Sunday mission, Lt Col Lowell Wallace, 238th RS Commander, said: "The mission was the genesis of a lot of work by multiple people in the 238th RS and even more across the 170th Group. Our new capability to generate independent weekend operations for Nebraska Air National Guard training is critical to keeping a combat ready force to assist 55th Wing missions both at home and abroad."

"Though we are proud to say that we accomplished the sortie using ANG [Air National Guard] personnel for launch, it of course takes the efforts of the entire 55 Wing team to make it happen from 55th Logistic Readiness Squadron transportation and fuel support, to 55th OSS airfield and tower management, to 55th Wing schedulers, to 55th Maintenance Group daily aircraft maintenance and to a whole host of Team Offutt professionals that keep the base running, it is truly a Total Force effort."

Above: **An RC-135 Rivet Joint takes-off from Al Udeid Air Base, Qatar.** USAF/SSgt Kylee Gardner

Below: **An RC-135 Rivet Joint uploads fuel from a KC-135 in the US Central Command area of responsibility.** USAF

JOLLY
GREEN II

Based at Moody Air Force Base, Georgia, the 41st Rescue Squadron has been in the combat search and rescue business with the HH-60 helicopter since 1989. This section looks at the mission, aircraft, and maintenance of this squadron.

Above:
Pararescuemen assigned to the 38th Rescue Squadron based at Moody Air Force Base, Georgia, conduct water rescue training in the Gulf of Mexico, on August 12, 2025.
USAF/TSgt Devin Boyer

AS THE US Air Force shifted its focus to rapidly manned small footprint contingency locations to maintain a strategic edge against enemies with advanced attack capabilities, so did its focus on conducting combat search and rescue. Based at Moody Air Force Base (AFB), Georgia, the 347th Rescue Group (RQG) regularly supports exercises focussed on readiness. One example is Mosaic Tiger, an exercise designed to hone a wing's ability to generate sorties while under simulated attack, with the potential scenario of having a downed aircraft and a hurt or captured pilot.

Explaining the ethos of the combat search and rescue (CSAR) mission, Col Brian Symon, 347th RQG commander, said: "We do everything in our power to find and recover isolated personnel anywhere on the globe. When they go to combat, they know that there is a community prepared to ensure that their worst day isn't their last day."

Training for CSAR missions tends to focus on tactical proficiency and technical skills, for example long-range rescue scenarios with restricted command and control capabilities, that require airmen to command the mission and operate in a disaggregated manner.

Explaining, Symon said: "We train for a variety of environments, conditions and events. We are accustomed to launching on dynamic missions and working with the rescue team to minimise risk while effecting the operation."

Tasks assigned to HH-60-equipped squadrons include humanitarian missions, civil search and rescue, disaster relief, casualty and medical evacuation (CASEVAC and MEDEVAC), and non-combatant evacuation operations.

Exercise Mosaic Tiger features different rescue scenarios, including overwater search and rescue, overland mass casualty recovery, and simultaneous rescue operations. Each event requires threat assessment, a game plan, and a quick response.

Mosaic Tiger is usually staged at Avon Park range with the rescue aircraft operating from Naval Air Station Key West. Both locations are in Florida but over 300 miles apart which replicates the tyranny of distance faced by CSAR crews in real combat zone rescues.

Underlining the reassurance rescue crews provide to other aircrews, Capt Matthew Helton, 347th Operations Support Squadron (OSS) and exercise planner, said: "CSAR also serves as a key safety net for any aircrew member who puts themselves in danger to accomplish a mission. There is a group of highly skilled and trained professionals dedicated to making sure they come home alive."

Referring to exercises like Mosaic Tiger, Capt Martinez-Alvarez said: "Training exercises stress the flow of standard communications allowing for tactical decisions to take place at the lowest level. Employing the commander's intent, CSAR aircrew can make decisions that impact the overall success or failure of their mission without the direct communication with higher leadership that we are used to operating with."

That's an important point because communications are likely to be interrupted when operating under the

Above: **An HH-60W Jolly Green II assigned to the 46th Expeditionary Rescue Squadron comes in for a landing during exercise Blue Phoenix in the US Central Command area of responsibility, on August 5, 2025.** USAF/A1C Keagan Lee

adaptive basing construct within the agile combat employment (ACE) concept of operations. Operating in unfamiliar territory behind enemy lines poses a challenging problem set for CSAR aircrews and the nearby rescue team.

The CSAR and personal recovery missions involve the rescue of personnel isolated from friendly forces and located behind enemy lines. These highly specialised missions are conducted by dedicated US Air Force rescue squadrons flying HC-130J Combat King II aircraft and HH-60W Jolly Green II helicopters operated by specially trained aircrews and pararescue personnel.

HH-60W Jolly Green II

The HH-60W Jolly Green II, dubbed the Whiskey, is gradually replacing the legacy HH-60G Pave Hawk, a type that has served Air Combat Command since it was created on June 1, 1992.

Then Secretary of State for Defense Mark Esper announced the HH-60W's name as Jolly Green II at the Air Force Association's Air Warfare Symposium on February 27, 2020. The name was chosen to honour the HH-3E and HH-53 helicopters dubbed as Jolly Green Giants during the Vietnam War, the pioneers of the CSAR mission.

Given the HH-60W's CSAR mission, which involves flying behind enemy lines, the hostility of that environment necessitates a suite of aircraft survivability equipment including an AAR-57(V)3 common missile warning system, ALE-47 countermeasures dispenser system, APR-52(V)1 radar warning receiver, and AVR-2B(V)1 laser detection system.

The HH-60W is also equipped with an upturned exhaust system, designed to reduce the helicopter's infrared signature, and armour for crew protection.

The cockpit is fitted with four multi-function displays with another three in the cabin. Avionics include a flight management system coupled with a flight director system, weather radar, an improved electro-optical/infrared camera, and over-the-horizon tactical data receivers capable of receiving near real-time mission and threat update information.

Mission systems include a Link-16 data link which enables integration with other platforms and combatant command nodes, an integrated broadcast receiver, a blue force tracker, and a personnel-locating system compatible with modern survival radios. The mission system integrates mission planning, mission computers, communications, sensors, and defensive systems, all supported by a faster data bus compared to the HH-60G.

Two external mounted gun systems with forward and side-firing capability can be fitted with crew-served weapons, specifically the GAU-2B/A 7.62mm six-barrel cannon, the GAU-18 0.50-calibre single-barrel heavy machine gun, and the GAU-21 0.50-calibre single-barrel rapid fire machine gun.

The HH-60W has a max gross take-off weight of 22,500lb, is capable flying in hot- and high-altitude environments and conduct an out-of-ground effect hover at its mid-mission gross weight at 4,000ft in a temperature up to 35°C.

The Whiskey is fitted with a new fuel system including a 660-gallon internal fuel tank giving a combat radius of 195nm without refuelling. Another benefit of the internal fuel tank's design is additional cabin space (compared to the HH-60G) which is optimised for the CSAR role and the adaptation for different tasks. An essential system for picking up friendly personnel isolated behind enemy lines is a hoist, the HH-60W is equipped with an externally mounted hoist with a 600lb capacity and 250ft of cable. The helicopter is also fitted with a cargo hook rated at 8,000lb capacity.

In terms of propulsion, the HH-60W is powered by two General Electric T700-GE-701D engines, driving four composite wide-chord main rotor blades, which fold to improve air transportation and shipboard operations.

Moody's Whiskey transition

The first pair of HH-60Ws was delivered to the 41st Rescue Squadron at Moody AFB, on November 5, 2020, starting the squadron's Whiskey transition.

Because the HH-60W has significantly more systems and automation compared to the HH-60G, it presents a steep learning curve to pilots new to the type, especially with the hand control.

The HH-60W's systems are all integrated, whereas the legacy HH-60G had a lot of separate boxes interfaced with each other. Consequently, the avionics shop had to understand different troubleshooting

methodology, and learn what system is located where.

Crew chiefs conduct daily maintenance, 40-hour inspections, and follow phase maintenance on a 42-day inspection interval.

The HH-60G was equipped with the Integrated Vehicle Health Management System (IVHMS), on the HH-60W the IVHMS is integrated into the aircraft – there are more sensors, so there are more data points and, consequently,

more data is generated. For certain faults that's beneficial, but with other faults, such as broken wires chafing, a person is required to inspect to find the fault. Despite the automation of fault diagnosis, crew chiefs state that the HH-60W is not easier to maintain than an HH-60G, Soundproofing covers a lot of the components that need to be inspected, so panels must be removed to access different parts of the helicopter.

Above: **HH-60W Jolly Green II 14-4488 taxis at Moody Air Force Base, Georgia on November 5, 2020, delivery day of the 41st Rescue Squadron's first two aircraft.** USAF/Andrea Jenkins

Left: **Airmen assigned to the 41st Rescue Squadron and pararescuemen assigned to the 38th Rescue Squadron, based at Moody Air Force Base, Georgia, conduct water rescue training in the Gulf of Mexico, on August 12, 2025.** USAF/TSgt Devin Boyer

Training

Learning the CSAR role is a tough challenge due to the variety of missions involved, so there is no 'one-size-fits-all' programme.

A unique aspect of the CSAR role is the need for helicopters and aircrew to be available, ready, and trained to execute with no notice in various complex mission sets. Simulation is used to good effect, US Air Force ranges are equipped with systems that simulate scenarios likely to be encountered on the battlefield, including Smokey SAMs (simulated missiles). Ground fire, surface-to-air missiles, and pop-up targets to shoot at are also simulated.

Participation in Exercise Red Flag at Nellis AFB, Nevada, provides aircrew the opportunity to be involved in the mission planning cycle and integration with each large strike package. Red Flag scenarios involve high-end threat environments and involve all types of aircraft, providing one of the highest and most complicated ways that CSAR can be presented to aircrews.

As a baseline, the threat level can be increased to replicate a battlespace from

Above: **A special missions aviator assigned to the 46th Expeditionary Rescue Squadron, stands ready for take-off during exercise Blue Phoenix in the US Central Command area of responsibility on August 5, 2025. This Exercise focuses on navigating the complex environment of personnel recovery, combat search and rescue, landing zone security and emergency medical care.** USAF/SrA Grace Turpin

Iraq, Syria, Yemen, or a peer environment, teaching CSAR aircrew how to work with an air force strike package, which is hugely complicated.

Attaining a level of training that reflects the reality of a CSAR pick-up is achieved by using control measures such as mission complexity, training in the local area to get comfortable with flying the aircraft, then to get used to employing the aircraft tactically, then to operate as a two-ship, then at night, then in one of the most challenging environments presented during Red Flag at Nellis, which involves flying around mountains and at high-density altitude.

One HH-60W pilot confessed that operating at 500ft and below on dark nights in a peacetime training scenario can be more uncomfortable than encountering enemy activity.

Pararescuemen

Critical members of an HH-60W crew are the pararescuemen (PJs) who recover and medically treat personnel who are isolated from friendly forces behind enemy lines. PJs are skilled parachutists, scuba divers, rock climbers, and are arctic trained. They serve with rescue squadrons manned only by PJs and take part in every aspect of a mission.

PJs frequently undertake full mission profile exercises that involve all the components of mission planning and mission execution, in different scenarios. One PJ said: "During mission planning, as a medic I look at all aspects of potential injuries and pose questions such as how long has the person been out there, and have they been fed? We prepare our gear and the equipment we foresee as necessary for the operation and the type of insertion

method and rig the helicopter to suit. We attend a briefing given by the team leader, who talks through the plan and how we're going to execute the mission.

"On the flight to the pick-up, we get in the mindset and go through the procedures. In some scenarios, you might have comms with the person while en route to them and sometimes you don't, but there are procedures to follow for specific scenarios. If you go down on the hoist, you're by yourself, or else you can go in with a team if necessary. You assess the casualty, apply life-saving treatment, and package the patient on a stretcher if they're ambulatory, while always being aware of any time constraint. You take direction from your team lead and commanders, move to the location and get the person loaded on the helicopter, then head out."

On October 4, 2022. Gen Mark Kelly, then commander of Air Combat Command, declared the HH-60W Jolly Green II had reached initial operational capability. This signified that the US Air Force had sufficient HH-60W helicopters, logistics requirements, and trained airmen to support a 30-day deployment to any independent location with a package of four aircraft.

Whiskeys in the Sonoran Desert

Air Combat Command's 355th Wing based at Davis-Monthan AFB, Arizona, is home to the second HH-60W unit, the 55th Rescue Squadron which received its first HH-60W Jolly Green II helicopter on May 3, 2023.

Col Scott Mills, then 355th Wing commander, said: "Rescue is more than a motto, it is a promise to every soldier, sailor, marine, airman and guardian that if you are ever isolated from friendlies, no amount of threat or distance will stop us from bringing you home. The Jolly Green II will help us keep that promise to our joint and coalition partners."

Sling load

The Moody-based 347th OSS conducted sling load training with a HH-60W Jolly Green II helicopter at the southern Georgia base on August 29, 2024. The event involved relocating cargo from one austere location to another, a capability that provides additional options to sustain forces in main operating bases, forward operating sites, and contingency locations. The event was an opportunity for air transportation airmen to be certified in rigging and directing sling-load operations. The 347th OSS conducts quarterly training to maintain high standards and proficiency in sling load operations.

First phase inspection

The 41st Rescue Generation Squadron began the first-ever phase inspection of an HH-60W Jolly Green II rescue helicopter on January 6, 2022. Undertaken on a 42-day interval, phase inspection serves as preventative maintenance and revealed how well the aircraft had stood up to its first 720 flight hours. Phase inspection is a more extensive and in-depth process than other inspections, and provides time for delayed maintenance issues to be completed, setting a benchmark for how inspection procedures will be done.

**Below:
Pararescuemen assigned to the 38th Rescue Squadron load a simulated patient into an HH-60W Jolly Green II at Moody Air Force Base on July 29, 2025. Pararescuemen performed tactical combat casualty care on a simulated patient before evacuation.**
USAF/A1C Savannah Carpenter

HILL LIGHTNINGS

The 388th Fighter Wing based at Hill Air Force Base, Utah, was the first Air Combat Command Wing to equip with the F-35A Lightning. Its three fighter squadrons and their fighter generation squadrons remain super busy.

AIRMEN FROM THE 388th Fighter Wing (FW) recently participated in an agile combat employment (ACE) exercise, flying and sustaining the F-35A Lightning II from various locations around the mountain states. The exercise dovetailed with Exercise Raging Gunfighter at Mountain Home Air Force Base (AFB), Idaho.

ACE concept forces units to manoeuvre and operate from a network of small, dispersed forward-operating locations and contingency locations with mission-ready airmen, contested logistics and a resilient, adaptable command and control structure. The intent is to complicate the enemies' targeting and increase survivability.

The 388th FW has been practicing and honing ACE with the F-35 for years, the evolution of the concept at an enterprise level, revised training requirements, and an influx of new airmen, mean the pursuit of improvements will never stop.

Col Michael Gette, 388th FW commander said: "This experience is new to many of our airmen. We need all of them to be prepared to fight and survive from anywhere, and alongside anyone, when we are called upon. Exercises like this give us some valuable field experience and expose our airmen to more realistic and more complex environments than they see day-to-day."

During the exercise, airmen from the 421st Fighter Squadron (FS) and Fighter Generation Squadron (FGS), alongside the 388th Operations Support Squadron (OSS), 388th Logistics Support Squadron (LSS), 388th Maintenance Squadron and 388th Munitions Squadron, operated aircraft from Hill AFB's alert facility, a contingency location across the flightline, Michael Army Airfield at Dugway Proving Ground, Utah, and from Mountain Home AFB.

To accomplish this, airmen from a variety of specialties were deployed to these locations as part of small Mission Ready Airmen teams. They quickly established the ability to receive, rearm, refuel and launch aircraft, as well as communicate with command elements.

Explaining the scenario, Technical Sergeant John-Barrett Ferreira, an inspection team member from the maintenance group said: "We want them to demonstrate their ability to survive in an unfamiliar environment with some chaotic injects thrown in, as well as operate functionally as a team and get these jets back in the fight. They have exercise constraints, and they've

got some real-world constraints, so they need to come together as a team to work through those."

Exercise Bamboo Eagle

Exercise Bamboo Eagle 25-1 was staged in February 2025. In preparation for the exercise, airmen from the 421st FS and 421st FGS moved a contingent of F-35A aircraft from Nellis AFB to Naval Air Station North Island, California, following the end of Exercise Red Flag 25-1. Bamboo Eagle is staged by the Nellis-based US Air Force Warfare Center with the objective of enhancing co-operation, agility, and combat readiness.

Bamboo Eagle is focused on providing the airpower needed to overcome pacing threats and disperses force elements and command and control structures to hub and spoke locations across the Western United States. Naval Air Station North Island served as a spoke where the airmen generated sorties with a small, flexible, movable team.

Pilots assigned to the 421st FS integrated with other aircraft from sister services, the Royal Air Force and the Royal Australian Air Force.

Explaining the necessity of Bamboo Eagle, US Air Force Air Warfare Center commander, Maj Gen Christopher Niemi said: "We have had the luxury of operating from safe-haven bases for many decades, and modern threats have fundamentally changed that reality. Bamboo Eagle helps us figure out how to manage those threats, and training together with our allies improves our ability to face those threats as a unified team."

Explaining the role played by maintainers assigned to the 421st FGS, Col Robert Kongaika, 388th Maintenance Group commander said: "During these exercises we operate at a scope much larger than we do on a day-to-day basis at Hill. Exercises like this are critical. It's that adage 'The more we

sweat in practice, the less we will bleed in battle'. If we exercise these movements to the point of failure, we will grow from it. These scenarios can be tough, but we're learning from them. We could be tasked with this at a moment's notice, and Bamboo Eagle is an experience our airmen will draw from."

In a hypothetical scenario requiring 'island hopping' from one airfield to the next, the smaller a maintenance team can be, the more mobile and survivable the entire operation is.

Explaining the maintenance output, Capt Tate Ashton, 388th Maintenance Group's tactics lead said: "We're working towards a concept where up to 80% of our core maintenance tasks can be done by anybody. So, all avionics, crew chiefs, weapons, munitions, and some back shops would be trained in these fundamentals.

"With every Airmen in a deployed squadron trained in the basic tasks required as a manoeuvre element, teams can be tailored to move forward from the hub to a spoke based on the manning and resources needed to meet the mission requirements in each location."

Providing an overview of the two exercises from a maintenance perspective, Master Sergeant Logan Schneider, 421st FGS Tactical Aircraft Maintenance NCOIC (Non-commissioned

Below: **An F-35A Lightning II aircraft assigned to the 421st Fighter Squadron returns to Naval Air Station North Island, California, following a Bamboo Eagle mission on February 10, 2025.** USAF/ Micah Garbarino

Officer in Charge) and Bamboo Eagle maintenance lead said: "For the 421st FGS, Red Flag 25-1 – which had a high operations tempo, but was less unpredictable than Bamboo Eagle – provided a good opportunity to build up some of the skills. Our crew chiefs are on the flightline all the time, but for the rest of our airmen, we got their hands on the jets, got them familiar with launching and recovering aircraft safely.

"For Bamboo Eagle, if our maintainers needed to move to an austere location on a C-130 or a helicopter, then we had a small team to refuel and rearm and launch sorties. Having more people trained gave us more flexibility."

Tough training

The flow of the daily flying schedule during Bamboo Eagle was driven by the different injects and tasking orders involved.

Discussing the complexities of the missions, Lt Col Bryan Mussler, 421st FS commander said: "Other exercises get our pilots used to working with others through the fog and friction of war, but not at the size and tempo of Bamboo Eagle. We've got pilots taking off, tasked with missions they weren't expecting, for much longer than they were expecting, and landing somewhere they weren't expecting. The unpredictability built into this exercise gives us a realistic look at what the fight will be like.

"We're trying to get somewhere between standard training and combat

experience. Our day-to-day training at home station is very low risk compared to the actual fight. Bamboo Eagle helps us bridge that gap to combat, so when that night comes, we are confident with what we're being tasked to do."

Most of the missions flown by the 421st FS involved offensive and defensive counter-air, escorting other aircraft and hunting down the enemy surface-to-air threats; the F-35's 'bread and butter' mission.

In addition to the combat scenarios, Bamboo Eagle is designed to improve the squadron's airmanship in piloting a single-engine fighter over the Eastern Pacific Ocean for great amounts of time and distance, meeting up with multiple tankers, navigating unfamiliar airspace, and landing at different airfields.

Explaining those aspects from a junior pilot's perspective, Lt Col Mussler said: "We have new F-35 pilots who have been with the squadron for two months and they've refuelled more this week than they ever have before, and in conditions they never have before. They're flying hundreds of miles out over the ocean, and you can't simulate that feeling. That makes it real for a lot of them. That realism is also motivating them, and they are having a lot of fun – solidifying the camaraderie we're going to need in combat."

Exercise Panther Shadow

In late April 2025, the 4th FS participated in a regional ACE exercise involving

F-35 flight operations from forward and contingency locations.

During the exercise, dubbed Panther Shadow, airmen assigned to the 4th FS and the 4th FGS, alongside the 388th OSS, 388th LSS, 388th Maintenance Squadron and 388th Munitions Squadron, generated aircraft from Hill, Mountain Home, and historic Wendover Airfield in Wendover, Nevada.

Airmen from a variety of specialties were deployed to the locations in small teams of mission-ready airmen, established the ability to receive, rearm, refuel and launch aircraft, and communicate with command elements.

Referring to the ACE operations, Col Michael Gette, 388th FW commander said: "This training prepares our airmen to integrate and carry out our mission to deliver F-35 dominance… anytime, anywhere."

A dispersed force structure complicates an enemy's targeting by making it difficult to locate and strike forward units, reducing the risk to traditionally more vulnerable steady-base infrastructure. Flexibility designed into agile combat operations, also allows commanders to adapt to a multitude of scenarios and conditions more rapidly.

This was the third regional ACE exercise the 388th FW had completed in the previous 12 months. The 34th and 421st FSs and their FGSs completed local exercises, Red Flag and Bamboo Eagle in 2024 and 2025. Throughout the summer of 2025, squadrons assigned to

Below: An F-35A Lightning II assigned to the 388th Fighter Wing at Hill Air Force Base, Utah, taxis after landing from a training sortie mission at the Utah test and training range on October 4, 2024. USAF/ Senior Airman Nicholas Rupiper

Above: **An F-35A Lightning II conducts a high-performance manoeuvre at Hill Air Force Base, Utah, during a practice performance by the display pilot assigned to the US Air Force F-35 Demonstration Team.** USAF/SSgt Kaitlyn Ergish

the 388th FW were deployed to Red Flag, the CENTCOM, and Indo-Pacific area of responsibility.

Training in the AFFORGEN Cycle

As part of the 388th FW's training plan, large force exercises like Red Flag at Nellis AFB, and Bamboo Eagle across the western United States, build upon local ACE exercises, which are built upon local flying and readiness days – with the intent of fielding a capable force within the Air Force Force Generation (AFFORGEN) cycle.

Discussing the AFFORGEN model, Col Charles Fallon, the current 388th FW commander, said: "Tempo, during the AFFORGEN cycle is of the utmost importance. You can't sprint to the starting line of a marathon. The certification phase is the culmination of a year's-worth of combat readiness generation. Throughout the previous 12 months, each squadron implements a training programme to gradually build unit and individual readiness, with an upward trajectory towards peak performance. That starts at Hill and continues towards complex off-station exercises that validate our readiness, certify units for combat, and provide feedback on areas where we need to improve."

Capstone Exercise

While the 34th and 421st FSs were deployed to the Indo-Pacific and CENTCOM areas of responsibility, the 4th FS returned from Red Flag and Bamboo Eagle, which helped prepare maintainers, support personnel and pilots for short-notice taskings anywhere in the world.

Discussing training, Lt Col Adam Thompson, 4th FS commander, said: "We do a lot of building-block type training daily at home station. While we're able to make it pretty complex and challenging, and even integrate other platforms and other units, we can't quite replicate the scale of Red Flag or Bamboo Eagle. And that scale is vital for training to the strengths of the F-35A and our core mission sets.

"One of the F-35's strengths is reducing the scale of the fight by being a force multiplier. A small number of F-35 aircraft can gather data from across the battlespace, share that information, employ against threats, while also making other fourth- and fifth-generation aircraft in the force package more effective. The platform has proven itself very capable in performing offensive and defensive counter-air, suppression of enemy air defences, escorting and protecting other aircraft."

Pilot upgrades

Explaining how squadron pilots gain experience and qualify for upgrades, Thompson said: "During Red Flag, the squadrons can focus on getting younger wingmen exposed to operating cooly and calmly in a high-threat environment that's saturated with other aircraft – both enemies and friendlies. They can also use mission planning opportunities to upgrade instructor pilots to mission commanders, who are then able to lead integrated force packages.

"During Bamboo Eagle, the focus shifts. The entire squadron, pilots and maintainers, are forced to operate in an agile combat employment environment across vast distances with degraded or contested logistics and communications. Decisions are driven down to lower levels and the entire unit mindset is focused on overcoming emerging challenges to ensure mission success.

"That's one of the most valuable things about these large exercises. We don't have the same distractions we have back at home station, and we can really start gelling as a mission generation force element – both ops and maintenance. Our communication and integration are tightening up at just the right time as we prepare to complete our training cycle."

SHAPING AND DEFINING THE FIGHT

Based at Tinker Air Force Base, Oklahoma, the E-3G-equipped 552nd Air Control Wing has been in the airborne command and control business since 1955. This section provides insight to the Wing's mission, aircraft, and maintenance.

FOR THE 552ND AIR Control Wing (ACW), the provision of intelligence from the battlespace to other aircraft and helicopters in the fight is its primary role. Explaining how intelligence shapes the battlespace, and how mission success begins long before take-off, Maj Alex Clawson, a senior intelligence officer with the 552nd ACW said: "We provide the combat intelligence cell team for all Red Flag participants. Essentially, we are the wing-level intel support for a wide array of mission design series aircraft spanning multiple nations. We support both mission planning and work directly with unit-level intel teams embedded in each squadron.

"A plan is only as good as the intelligence behind it. To craft an effective strategy, you must understand how your adversary operates. That is where intelligence preparation of the battlespace comes in. We lay the groundwork for the entire mission planning process."

Red Flag emphasises joint and coalition warfare, requiring seamless integration

between branches and allied nations. The Red Flag 25-2 provided an opportunity for intelligence professionals to see how different forces operate.

Discussing Red Flag 25-2, Clawson said: "Each service employs intelligence slightly differently. The navy and marines, for example, utilise unit-level intel in ways that differ from the air force. It is not a matter of right or wrong. It is just different. Red Flag 25-2 provided a great learning experience for us and an opportunity to help our coalition partners refine how they support their platforms."

Terminology was one of the biggest challenges, as Clawson explained: "Words mean different things to different services. Red Flag is an air force-led exercise, so our navy and coalition partners had to adapt to our analytical processes and terminology. At the same time, we had to learn how they approach problem-solving, and establish a common language to include acronyms."

The Nellis core intelligence cell was not directly embedded with the command-and-control (C2) units during Red Flag, but their impact was undeniable. The teams have squadron-level intel, but they were not embedded during execution. Explaining, Clawson said: "C2 teams make the tough calls in battle management. But those decisions are only as good as the intelligence they are based on. Whether it is a marine, sailor, or airman running C2, their ability to make informed decisions in combat hinges on accurate, timely intel."

For the younger airmen assigned to the 552nd's intel team, Red Flag 25-2 was the first time they had supported a variety of aircraft types, their crew seeing first-hand how each platform prioritises intelligence. At the conclusion of their participation in Red Flag, the airmen had achieved a deeper understanding of joint and coalition operations, and interoperability.

Defining victory at Red Flag

Staged three times per year at Nellis Air Force Base (AFB), Nevada, Exercise Red Flag always involves E-3G Sentry aircraft assigned to the 552nd ACW. By its design, Red Flag simulates a large-scale conflict, in which C2 plays a vital role. According to the 552nd ACW, C2 is the lifeblood of modern warfare, without which, the fight cannot happen.

Discussing the importance of C2, Capt Benisha Simpson, an air battle manager assigned to the 963rd Airborne Air Control Squadron (AACS), said: "Aircrews see the fight, the dogfights, the missile launches, but they don't see us. They don't realise that none of it happens without us directing, co-ordinating, and making sure that every moving part functions as a whole."

Simpson was referring to an invisible force of personnel that bind every operation together: air battle managers, weapons directors, intelligence analysts, and in the case of Red Flag, marine air support operators controlling aircraft disjointed around the exercise airspace into a lethal force.

Explaining a Red Flag scenario, air battle manager, Lt Melanie Wittick said: "We are the chessboard, the pilots flying in the air battle are the chess pieces. Without us, there's no strategy, just pieces moving blindly across the board. At the heart of the air battle is the E-3G Airborne Warning and Control System which provides real-time battlefield awareness acting as the eyes and ears of the fight, detecting threats, and directing friendly forces to engage or evade."

Commenting, Capt Patrick Ford, an air battle manager assigned to the 963rd AACS said: "Pilots can only see what's in front of them. We see everything. We see the whole battlespace and tell the pilots what they can't see, what's beyond their radar range, what's manoeuvring to kill them, and how to avoid it."

US Marine Corps air support squadrons mirror this function on the ground, providing C2 capabilities from tactical operations centres. Capt Justin Young, executive officer of Air Defense Company Bravo, Marine Air Support Squadron 2 (MASS-2), described their role as ensuring that fighters can operate safely, manage traffic, and battle-track threats beyond visual range.

LCpl Alia Green, an air support operator assigned to Marine Air Support Squadron 3, (MASS-3) spent Red Flag conducting surveillance and maintaining airspace awareness. She described the challenge of monitoring aircraft movements and ensuring that flight paths remained deconflicted in the chaos of battle. Her previous experience in virtual simulations like Coalition Virtual Flag had helped her grasp the fundamentals, but nothing compared to doing it live. "So much happens at once. You must process information fast. You must be right. A mistake could mean a mid-air collision, or worse, striking friendly forces," she said.

According to the 552nd ACW, the difference between winning and losing a

Below: **An E-3 Sentry assigned to the 965th Expeditionary Airborne Air Control Squadron taxies on the runway at Al Udeid Air Base, Qatar.** USAF/MSgt Jennifer Calhoun

Johnson said: "We study everything. We track what the enemy does. We look at their patterns. The more we know, the better prepared we are. The more our pilots know, the better their chances of surviving."

Red Flag is designed in a way that allows mistakes to be made in the training, the objective being that mistakes don't happen in combat. For participating C2 teams, Red Flag scenarios evolve in real-time, pushing the teams to react under pressure. Each mission builds on the one before, increasing in complexity until the exercise culminates in a full-scale war scenario.

Explaining, Capt Ford said: "We're not just practising tactics, we're training decision-making. We're training our ability to process information, to communicate clearly, and to execute under pressure. That's what wins wars."

Emphasising C2's irreplaceable role in air combat, Col Kenneth Voigt, then 552nd ACW commander, said: "America does not go into combat without air power, and air power cannot happen without battle management command and control provided by our airmen. By the end of a Red Flag exercise, trust is no longer a question but an expectation. The pilots know that when they check in, someone is watching their back. The controllers know that the information they provide will be acted on without

fight is decision superiority. Information moves from ground-based intelligence cells to airborne command centres, then to the fighters and bombers executing the mission. Every decision is based on a constant data flow, tracking friendly forces, enemy positions, and threats that emerge without warning.

Lt Mackenzie Mack, the weapons tactics officer in charge at MASS-2, emphasised the importance of trust. "Red Flag brought together units that had never worked with one another before, forcing marines, airmen, sailors, and coalition partners to operate as a single team. We had to learn how to communicate. If we don't trust each other, people die. It's that simple. Trust also defines the relationship between pilots and controllers. In the cockpit, a fighter pilot sees only what is immediately ahead. They rely on

Above: **An airman marshals an E-3 Sentry at Al Udeid Air Base, Qatar during a rotational deployment to the US Central Command area of responsibility.** USAF/SSgt Michael Means

command and control to clear the battle and guide them toward threats and away from danger," she said.

Capt Jewell Smith, section lead for a crew assigned to the 728th Battle Management Control Squadron, described the job as providing a second set of eyes for the pilots. "They're expecting to hear us," Smith said. "They need us. If they don't hear a voice on the radio, if they don't have that situational awareness, they're flying blind. They don't know what's coming."

For intelligence teams, their job starts before the fight begins. Airman Jayden Johnson, an intelligence specialist, builds situational awareness before aircraft even leave the ground. His job involves analysing enemy tactics, movements, and potential threats, to ensure that pilots go into battle with an edge. Explaining,

hesitation. The intelligence teams know that their analysis shapes the fight before it begins. The battle doesn't start in the cockpit. It starts in the unseen world of command and control, where information becomes action, and chaos becomes victory."

Tinker: home of the E-3G Sentry

The 552nd ACW first arrived at Tinker from the then McClellan AFB, California, in July 1976. Throughout its tenure at the Oklahoma super base, it has operated the Boeing E-3 Sentry, the original airborne warning and control system dubbed AWACS. The wing comprises four groups.

552nd Air Control Group is responsible for ground-based command and control. Two squadrons are assigned. The 752nd Operation Support Squadron and the 552nd Air Control Network Squadron, the latter provides cyber defence of the wing's weapons systems and supports ground-based cyber equipment for the AWACS.

552nd Maintenance Group (MXG) comprises the Maintenance Squadron, the Aircraft Maintenance Squadron, and the Logistics Support Squadron. It trains junior maintainers arriving at the wing from tech school at Sheppard AFB, Texas.

552nd Operations Group (OG) has four flying squadrons assigned, the 960th, 963rd, 964th and 965th AACC, and an operational support squadron. The 552nd OG supports multiple combatant commands.

552nd Training Group consists of two training squadrons, the 436th Training Squadron based at Dyess AFB, Texas, responsible for training aircrew flight equipment individuals in the air force, and the 966th AACS, conducting initial qualification, mission qualification, and instructor upgrade training for all ten crew positions on the E-3G, and the 552nd Training Support Squadron (TSS) conducts academic training and manages the flow of more than 500 permanent-party and temporary duty (TDY) students annually.

There are two other E-3 Sentry squadrons in the air force, the 961st AACS based at Kadena Air Base, Okinawa, and the 962nd AACS based at Elmendorf AFB, Alaska, each assigned to their respective wing. The 552nd MXG supports both units with deep maintenance.

The 552nd ACW maintains a detachment of maintainers, operators, and cyber specialists at RAAF Base Williamtown, New South Wales, with No.2 Squadron which will form the seed corn cadre of individuals that will introduce the E-7 to the US Air Force.

Explaining the wing's name, Voigt said: "The US does not go into combat without air power. We learned that lesson in World War One. We know how to conduct combat with air power. Our joint tactics are built upon air power and the ability to gain and maintain some semblance of air security and be able to control the skies. That does not happen without battle management command and control. Our job is to control the skies and make sure that air assets are where they need to be. This is the only wing in the Department of Defense that is solely focused on battle management and command and control from the ground [control and reporting centre – CRC] and from the air [AWACS]. Without the 552nd, we don't have air control, we don't have air power and America doesn't go to war. That's the importance we try to hammer home to our airmen on how important their job is, and why we call ourselves America's Wing."

Discussing the wing's training objective, Voight said: "Our objective is to make sure that leaders throughout the wing and all levels are able to operate in a forward and deployed environment, because that's where they'll operate from. We want to make sure our leaders understand intent, how to take action, how to take care of their people, and

Below: **E-3G Sentry, serial number 76-1607/OK, painted with a red tail stripe of the 964th Air Control and Command Squadron, lands on the main runway at Tinker Air Force Base.**
Mark Ayton

most importantly, how to have difficult conversations with their people. Our big focus during the last calendar year has been an initiative called 'the road to ready'. It's about getting us ready for the pacing challenge. The E-3 has been in CENTCOM [US Central Command] for a very long time, and it's a very important mission, but when you go to fight a peer adversary, it's a different mission.

"In asymmetric warfare we have air superiority, cyber security, space superiority, which means there are things that battle managers don't have to think about, but in a peer competition they will have to think about being contested in the air, space, and cyber domains, and logistic channels, and how we deliver air power to the Joint Force Commander.

"In a recent edition of Exercise Bamboo Eagle, staged off the west coast of the United States, our ability to conduct agile combat employment, logistics and command and control were all stressed. With our ground-based command and control agencies forward deployed to the islands off San Diego, and our aircraft at Harry Reid International Airport, Las Vegas, our ability to launch aircraft was stressed because they were not at their main hub, and we had to make sure they could logistically launch on the ATO [air tasking order] timeline from a different base. The team achieved ten out of ten launches over a five-day exercise with a short turn time between sorties each day.

They launched two sorties a day, every day, with just two aircraft.

"The ground-based command and control units deployed the new Tactical Operation Center-Light system with two C-130s. It took two days to set up and was broken down in under 40 minutes. The lift requirement for the entire squadron on a combat deployment required 23 C-17s."

Explaining the amount of equipment, Col Andrew Babiarz, commander, 552nd Air Control Group, said: "The current equipment load out of our control and reporting centres comprises multiple five-ton trucks that require a significant amount of C-17 to move the

team with a typical 180-person UTC [Unit Type Code – a capability focused on accomplishing a specific mission] to set up a control site out in the field. We achieved that with ten people and a couple of pickup trucks transported on two C-130s. That is what's required to be agile and mobile in a modern battle space. Our ability to move quickly and be responsive to the combatant commander, has always been a core tenet for the control and reporting centre to be able to move around the battle space, set up and function as a static, persistent, C2 capability.

"Over time, our equipment load grew bigger, which slowed us down. As

Right: **An E-3G Sentry undergoes pre-flight checks at Nellis Air Force Base, Nevada, during Bamboo Eagle to ensure the aircraft is ready for its command-and-control mission.** USAF/ Garrett Cole

Below: **An E-3 Sentry over Afghanistan back in 2011.** USAF/MSgt Willian Greer

Right: **Crew chiefs drag chocks to a parking spot as an E-3 Sentry taxies to parking at Al Udeid Air Base, Qatar.** USAF/SSgt Michael Means

Below: **Painted with a multi-colour tail stripe and marked 552 ACW, is the current flagship aircraft for the wing commander.** Mark Ayton

we look at peer and near peer threat environments and what the future of warfare might be, we realised we had to reduce our equipment load by taking advantage of smaller technologies, which allows us to move quicker. We're experimenting with new kit to determine what our final load will be. None of that kit is Program of Record [PoR – an acquisition plan], fully operational capability hardware. It is experimental kit that we're letting our airmen figure out its best utilisation. We're down to a handful of Pelican cases. We think we can do better by using different types of kit to make us smaller, lighter, and more lethal to a point now we're experimenting in major exercises in a span of two years."

Explaining how the wing is changing the employment of the E-3, Col James Ord, commander, 552nd Training Group, said: "What we expect of our flight deck and mission crews has changed. As the threats have evolved, we are evolving. Part of our road to ready initiative is how we execute inside a theatre of operation with a basic threat. We have changed how the flight crew manoeuvres the aircraft and where they position the aircraft to survive, we've changed what the mission crew communicates to fighters, and we've changed our sims to reflect that, so it's second nature to our aircrew and our mission crew. We're about 15 months into this new training programme, and we're getting to where we need to be in order to make sure that our tactics are solid, and our crews know what we expect from them.

"The air battle managers are able to tell the flight crew where the threat is, and how to manoeuvre and position the aircraft, without manoeuvring the aircraft in such a way where we would lose the ability to conduct the mission at an acceptable level of risk."

Discussing the aircraft's viability, Col Jason Zemler, former commander 552nd OG, said: "There's a lot of discussion about the viability of the E-3 airframe in the Pacific fight. We don't operate alone. We are part of a force package that provide indications and threat warnings so we can place the aircraft to maintain survivability and contribute where we can, and then retrograde when we need to. We've adjusted our training plan to focus on an adversary that now wants to kill me with the capability and the intent to do so. How do I move my airframe to put myself in a position of advantage? Through exercises like Bamboo Eagle [see later] and other events, we're learning what that looks like on our way to the E-7 and figuring out how the E-7 will be additive in that process."

Explaining how an E-3 is employed in a large exercise to reflect combat, Zemler said: "The air force as an enterprise is adjusting and open to feedback from the weapon systems that need to maintain viability. That's achieved by employing the latest tactics and techniques that put the weapon system in a position of advantage for how we think we would employ in combat.

But it depends on the exercise and what the primary training objective is, which for Red Flag is creating package commanders in the fighter force, who can run the package and get bombs on target, on time.

"In Bamboo Eagle, instead of being a training aid to the primary training audience, we were part of the primary training audience, so we drove more of the desired learning objectives to the point where we outlined what we can provide to the fight, how we can build the primary and emergency C2 plan, and how we can make sure the Joint Force Commander gets what they need in that environment."

At the start of the E-3 divestment programme there were seven different aircraft configurations on the ramp which added to the training burden. Today, across the fleet, there is one aircraft configuration that receives minor software updates and minor crypto updates which are easy to manage. Training is now focused on the one aircraft configuration.

Discussing the rationalisation to aircraft configuration, Col Casey Stevens, former commander 552nd MXG, said: "When we make decisions on how we're going to upgrade, we have to determine the timing. We had to align the aircraft modifications with aircrew training to ensure they were certified to fly aircraft configured in a certain way. As an enterprise we decided to get all the aircraft upgraded as quickly as possible."

Summing up, Voight said: "Following 20 years of fighting the global war on terror, we're now training our folks to be able to make decisions at the speed of an information battlefield, take the commander's intent and make decisions to enact combat, which is a huge lift for everyone."

Tactical Operation Centre - Light

The 752nd Operations Support Squadron (OSS) is experimenting with a smaller and more mobile version of the legacy Control and Reporting Center called the Tactical Operation Center-Light (TOC-L). According to the 552nd ACW, TOC-L offers transformative communication capabilities, with the ability to operate in multiple locations on the battlefield.

The 752nd OSS is Air Combat Command's pathfinder unit, tasked to experiment with the kits at major exercises such as Bamboo Eagle, to refine requirements for the next round of prototypes.

As part of its tasking, the 752nd OSS is developing tactics, techniques and procedures and the equipment to rapidly execute kill webs, which integrate all joint fire control networks or translate between them.

Flight deck, engine start and take-off

US Air Force E-3 aircraft underwent a flight deck avionics upgrade known as DRAGON (Diminishing manufacturing sources Replacement of Avionics for Global Operations and Navigation). DRAGON ensures compliance with current and future air traffic control requirements in international and domestic airspace which enables crews access to RVSM (Reduced Vertical Separation Minimum) airspace and optimal flight levels to increase fuel efficiency.

Analogue technology on the flight deck was replaced with digital flight management systems that includes five multi-colour graphic displays that customise and accurately portray engine, navigation and radar data, mode-5 IFF (identification friend or foe and ADS-B (automatic dependent surveillance – broadcast). The first E-3G aircraft upgraded with DRAGON arrived at Tinker in January 2017.

Describing use of the system, Maj Samantha Eilish, an aircraft commander, said: "The DRAGON systems provide pilots with more situational awareness in the air and in the event of an emergency. For most emergencies, an annunciation pops up, either red or yellow, depending on the severity. The alerts pop-up quickly so we can act on it faster."

Given the necessity of the E-3's mission to US airpower, planning any mission is a multi-faceted process that takes place the day prior when the entire crew assembles to plan the mission and discuss its requirements.

Providing more insight to the mission planning, Eilish said: "We speak with various fighter squadrons to find out what their training needs are and whether we can meet those needs and include them in our plan. If we're fortunate to operate with fighter aircraft during a training mission, we'll operate in a dedicated orbit area, airspace safe from other traffic, from where we'll support and control the fighters."

Technical Sergeant Zach Kruly is an evaluator flight engineer who is usually the first member of the aircrew to go out to the aircraft to conduct the pre-flight checks. Explaining the process, Kruly said: "This starts with the initial walk around, and make sure all the flight deck systems

Below: **An E-3 Sentry seen on take-off from Al Dhafra Air Base, United Arab Emirates during a bi-lateral exercise with the UAE Air Force.** USAF/MSgt Wolfram Stumpf

the air-cooling system. After the checklist is complete, I increase the rotordome to transit speed and ultimately full speed to achieve full radar sweep. The rotordome starts spinning at engine start. It has multiple speeds. The first one is called idle, which is a quarter rotation per minute. Turning the rotordome dampens vibration created by the engines which can damage the bearings on the rotordome if it is not turning and ensures we don't have any flat spots."

Explaining the effects of the rotordome on the aircraft's handling, Eilish said: "The airframe was designed for the rotordome to be aerodynamically neutral, so the aircraft is balanced in such a way that a coefficient of drag through the rotordome isn't supposed to add any actual applicable feel to the pilots themselves. When flying the approach and landing, you're constantly adjusting the throttles.

are powered up so that when the pilots arrive on the flight deck, they have nothing more to do than speak to the maintainers as required."

Detailing the processes completed prior to engine start, Eilish said: "Before engine starts, we make sure our screens are displaying the data we need for take-off. Typically, if something's showing as an issue, we co-ordinate with maintenance. During the ground phase of the mission and on take-off, engine instrumentation is the primary display we're watching to make sure everything's within limitations because if not, we're going to return to get it fixed. The DRAGON avionics provides a warning enunciator on the centre display. Engine start is in the order 3-4-2-1 and is overseen by a crew chief out on the flight line.

"At the runway, the flight engineer pushes the engine levers forward to the power required, which allows me to focus on making the aircraft as safe and stable as possible during the take-off sequence during which I'm cross checking, looking outside to make sure we're on centre line, and then looking at my instruments to make sure everything's in the green. I go back and forth between those, until we get to V2 [take-off safety speed] and then rotate at V1 [decision speed]."

Discussing the procedures further, Kruly said: "During climb out, provided there are no issues with the airframe, the aircraft commander will call for the after-take-off checklist which the flight engineer starts to work through. It's my job to start powering up the mission systems which need cooling, so I turn on

Above: USAF/ SSgt Justin Parsons

Right: **A flight engineer conducts preflight checks onboard an E-3G Sentry during Bamboo Eagle at Nellis Air Force Base, Nevada. The 552nd ACW played a critical role in ensuring the E-3 aircraft is mission-ready for the large-scale exercise, which tests the integration of multiple air and ground assets.** USAF/Garrett Cole

Right: **An airborne data systems technician assigned to the 965th Airborne Air Control Squadron, conducts pre-flight checks onboard an E-3G Sentry during Bamboo Eagle. The 965th AACS held a pivotal role in the exercise maintaining data integrity and system functionality.** USAF/Garrett Cole

You try and set your known power setting, of course, but depending on weather and winds, you must invariably fine tune it."

Explaining procedures after landing, Kruly said: "Once on the parking spot, the first thing we want to do is shut down the engines. During the taxi the pilot powers-up the APU [auxiliary power unit] to supply power to the aircraft and its mission systems, and provide bleed air for air conditioning. We don't need four engines running for safety reasons, so we shut down the outboard engines. Leaving the inboard engines running helps with fault diagnosis of any issue encountered during the flight."

Formal training unit

The 966th AACS is the E-3 Sentry formal training unit with the primary role of flight instruction and evaluation. Explaining the tasking, Lt Col Jacob Dykstra, deputy commander 966th AACS, and an air battle manager evaluator, said: "We instruct pilot, flight engineer, computer, radar and radio technicians, air battle managers and mission system operators.

"Students arrive at the 966th after completing their initial training to earn their wings with the 337th Air Control Squadron based at Tyndall AFB, Florida. The 337th trains officers to become air battle managers. They start with the academics' phase with the 52nd TSS and then complete the flight phase with the 966th."

Discussing the 52nd's role, its assistant director of operations, Maj Michael Swanson, said: "Students

Above: **The edge of the rotordome shows the wear and tear of an aircraft originally procured in 1977 and long out of programme depot maintenance.**
Mark Ayton

study sensor theory and operation in the academics' phase. Daily classes are then paired with a simulator session to provide plenty of touch time with the system before they start the flying phase. Our simulator comprises several consoles spatially arranged in a room but doesn't look or feel like you're on an aircraft but is effective.

"Initial qualification is about knowing how to use the weapon system. Can you flip the switches and push the buttons? Do you know where things are? Do you know the basic procedures and checklists? Then students must apply that skill set to specific missions, so we'll put them in a variety of notional missionised scenarios involving other agencies and assets.

"All training in the flying phase is undertaken as part of a crew, but the crew is not tasked. Students are paired with an instructor and are not allowed to operate on their own. When crewed with students and instructors, the jet can execute any task that an operational squadron could undertake, but with a lot of instructors alongside the students.

"A unique challenge of training the command-and-control role is the context of the combat operating environment. When you fly around the United States on any day, none of that context is present, and we can't easily generate other real-world assets together in one place. That can only be created in a simulator environment. That's why students return to the simulator

environment for mission qualification training [MQT] after they've completed the flying phase, to reapply the skills learned to this point in a rigorous missionised context.

"They're training for a mission set, working as a crew. Knowing what another crew member is doing and how they can be utilised, MQT brings that all together, for which students should be able to identify a possible problem, what to do about the problem, and who to turn to for support. Run by the 52nd TSS, MQT is a 15-day course, which students must pass before they are patched onto their first operational squadron.

"Each crew position has a different syllabus with a different tolerance for how many missions students need to conduct in the air before they go on to their qualification event. Anywhere from four to 13 specific to the requirements of that crew position. If you're in a crew position that's one deep, meaning there's only one person on the jet that does that job, you'll do more events in the air prior to the qualification event."

Mission crew

Onboard and E-3 aircraft, members of the mission crew operate from dedicated consoles at the front and aft of the mission cabin, and from one of the console banks labelled the front bank, the command bank positioned over wing, or the back bank.

The mission crew comprises the following crew positions:

An airborne radio operator has responsibility to set up, operate, maintain, troubleshoot, and shut down all the radios used by the mission crew over the course of a flight.

An airborne data systems technician has responsibility for the mission system computers (one does the raw processing, one handles all the interfacing), the interfaces between the radar, the passive detection system, the links, and tactical chat.

Air battle managers (officers), also known as section leads, oversee crew members and co-ordinate with the flight deck crew, work in conjunction with mission system operators (enlisted) in battle management teams. A battle management team is scalable and tailorable based on the mission set assigned.

Mission system operators configure the data link systems that allow machine-to-machine communication, so information is displayed as an integrated track that enables the operator to do tactical command and control. Their primary task is to detect, identify and track aircraft.

A section lead in charge (SLIC) is responsible for ensuring the aircraft is in position to employ on time, on station, and for co-ordination with the flight deck about any safety concerns. A SLIC has overall responsibility for monitoring all the battle management teams (BMTs) to ensure they are operating correctly, and the systems are running.

An airborne radar technician is responsible for activating the radar, running tests to ensure it is functioning efficiently and correctly, and is not harmful to the crew in any way.

Bamboo Eagle

Exercise Bamboo Eagle is a recent edition to Air Combat Command's annual series of large force exercise. In the third edition of the series in FY2024, dubbed Bamboo Eagle 24-3, the 552nd ACW participated as a combat wing for the first time with nine mission generation force elements (MGFEs) integrated in one Air Expeditionary Wing (AEW).

The exercise tested the wing's ability to execute long-range kill chains, to demonstrate the paradigm shift in how C2ISREW (Command, Control, Intelligence, Surveillance, Reconnaissance, and Electronic Warfare) assets are nested under a single combat wing.

Operating from six locations under the agile combat employment concept (ACE) of operation, the 552nd ACW's performance in Bamboo Eagle informed air force re-optimisation and the shape of future C2ISR Combat Wings.

Like all editions of Bamboo Eagle, 24-3 was billed as a crucible for airmen to sharpen their skills against the formidable challenges of the pacing threat of tomorrow. Far from routine, the joint exercise tested personnel and their weapon systems technology.

According to the news release issued by the 552nd ACW, the wing's performance in Bamboo Eagle 24-3 was set to inform air force re-optimisation and directly shape the future of C2ISR combat wings. As units of action, combat wings will be critical in meeting the air force's pacing challenge [China], ensuring that the 552nd ACW continues to deliver Battle Management Command and Control (BMC2) across high-level training exercises like Cope North and Red Flag — preparing operators, maintenance, and support personnel for conflict in the Indo-Pacific.

Below: **E-3G Sentry, serial number 76-1604/OK, painted with a red tail stripe of the 964th Air Control and Command Squadron, undergoing maintenance on the flight line at Tinker Air Force Base.** Mark Ayton

Capt Michael Seitz, maintenance lead for Bamboo Eagle 24-3, said: "The exercise represented more than just a tactical drill. It embodied the air force's evolving approach to warfare. Bamboo Eagle is a newer exercise that builds on lessons learned over decades of Red Flag. This takes it to a whole new level by integrating new TTPs [tactics, techniques and procedures] so that we can go forward in the future fight, compete, and ultimately win."

Seitz oversees the indispensable E-3G Sentry aircraft which remains a critical asset despite its years in service. Describing the aircraft, Seltz said: "The E-3 Sentry is an ageing platform and it's easy to see that it's on its way out, but the capabilities it brings to the fight are still very relevant. We have a wing full of operators that work tirelessly to perfect their trades and we still bring a lot to the fight."

Outlining the importance of seemingly small tasks contributing to the mission's success, Senior Airman Edward McCue, a metals technologist for the 552nd ACW, said: "We often deal with stuck screws, and while that might sound minor, a single screw can ground an entire aircraft. It's a reminder that even the smallest details matter in ensuring mission success. Just like a stuck screw can delay a flight, each of us, no matter our position, plays a role in the success or failure of the mission. That's what Bamboo Eagle reinforces."

Highlighting the importance of the integration at Bamboo Eagle, 552nd OG commander Zemler said: "This exercise brings together elements from nearly every Major Command in the air force and it was a rare opportunity to see how we function as a cohesive unit against a pacing threat in a live environment."

DRONE-BASED ISR

A review of the MQ-9 Reaper and RQ-4 Global Hawk uncrewed aircraft used by the US Air Force for the intelligence, surveillance, and reconnaissance role.

AN OFFICIAL US Air Force definition of intelligence, surveillance, and reconnaissance (ISR) lists the capability as, "the foundation upon which every joint interagency, and coalition operation achieves success."

The ISR role involves the acquisition, processing and provision of timely, accurate, relevant, coherent, and assured information and intelligence to support the conduct of military operations during peacetime and war, providing a combatant commander with the so-called decision advantage.

This section focusses on the manned and uncrewed aircraft operated by the US Air Force used for the ISR mission.

Most manned and uncrewed US Air Force aircraft used for the ISR role are assigned to five active-duty wings: the 9th Reconnaissance Wing at Beale Air Force Base (AFB), California (U-2S Dragon Lady, *see p30*), the 55th Wing at Offutt AFB, Nebraska (RC-135 family, *see p70*), 319th Reconnaissance Wing at Grand Forks AFB, North Dakota (RQ-4B Global Hawk), the 432nd Wing at Creech

AFB, Nevada (MQ-9 Reaper), and the 552nd Air Control Wing at Tinker AFB, Oklahoma (E-3G Sentry, *see p96*). All five wings are part of Air Combat Command headquartered at Langley AFB, Virginia.

Air Combat Command is known as an institutional command with the responsibility for providing combat airpower to combatant commands, primarily (but not limited to) US Central Command (Southwest Asia), US European Command (EUCOM), and US Indo-Pacific Command (USINDOPACOM).

Provision of combat airpower to a combatant command requires aircraft to deploy from the home station to an overseas base located in the area of responsibility (AOR). This takes several forms.

Some ISR aircraft are deployed and operated by a squadron permanently based in the AOR. An example is the 95th Reconnaissance Squadron (RS) based at RAF Mildenhall, England, which operates RC-135 aircraft in the US European Command AOR. MQ-9 and RQ-4 aircraft are also operated by squadrons permanently based in the AOR.

By comparison, when RC-135 aircraft deploy to the US Central Command (CENTCOM) AOR they are assigned to and operated by an expeditionary squadron assigned to an air expeditionary wing (AEW) for the duration of the TDY (temporary duty). Expeditionary wings and squadrons operate under temporary orders for a specific objective and are inactivated once the objective is complete. The current mix of AEWs operating in the CENTCOM AOR have been in existence for the past two decades. When deployed to the CENTCOM AOR, MQ-9 and RQ-4 aircraft are also operated by an expeditionary squadron assigned to an AEW for the duration of the TDY.

Grand Forks, Grand Missions

The 319th Reconnaissance Wing is the host unit at Grand Forks which conducts the high altitude ISR mission and operates the nation's high frequency global communication system. The 319th Operations Group (OG) oversees the infrastructure and support for round-the-clock RQ-4 missions across the globe. It oversees two geographically separated units providing launch and recovery for RQ-4 operations: the 4th RS at Anderson AFB, Guam, and the 7th RS at Naval Air Station Sigonella, Sicily.

Commenting on RQ-4 operations from Sigonella, Maj Benjamin Buckley, assistant director of operations for the 7th RS, said: "The primary mission is launching, recovering and providing sorties for the RQ-4 Block 40 aircraft in support of EUCOM, AFRICOM and CENTCOM missions."

Explaining the mission, Lt Col David Hind, commander of the 7th RS, said: "We provide 24/7 non-stop intelligence, surveillance, and reconnaissance support in EUCOM, CENTCOM and AFRICOM (US Africa Command). The Global Hawk allows us the capability to pilot the

Below: **An RQ-4 Global Hawk under tow along the flight line at Grand Forks Air Force Base, North Dakota, home station of the 319th Reconnaissance Wing.** USAF/ SrA Elora McCutcheon

Left: **An RQ-4 Global Hawk undergoes maintenance on the flight line at Grand Forks Air Force Base, North Dakota. The Global Hawk is a high-altitude, long-endurance, remotely piloted aircraft with an integrated sensor suite that provides global all-weather, day or night intelligence, surveillance, and reconnaissance capability.** USAF/SrA Elora McCutcheon

aircraft from anywhere in the world. We maintain a pilot presence here locally to command the aircraft during take-offs and landings and then we can pass control to pilots flying at the home station at Grand Forks Air Force Base."

RQ-4 Global Hawk

The RQ-4B Global Hawk is a high-altitude, long-endurance, all-weather, day/night ISR uncrewed aircraft system. The US Air Force procured four different variants designated Block 10 (pre-production standard), Block 20, Block 30, and Block 40, each with a different level of capability. Following years of disagreement with the Congress about the retirement of the RQ-4 Global Hawk

system, the US Air Force finally divested its Block 20 aircraft during FY2021, followed by its Block 30 aircraft during FY2022. Today 11 Global Block 40 aircraft remain in service with Air Combat Command's 319th Reconnaissance Wing based at Grand Forks AFB.

Block 40 is a ground-moving target surveillance platform equipped with the ZPY-2 X-band Multiplatform Radar Technology Insertion Program (MP-RTIP), an active electronically scanned array (AESA) radar capable of detecting both moving and static targets. The system consists of the aircraft and sensors, a launch and recovery element (LRE), a mission control element (MCE), and a comms/mission planning cell.

To deliver survivable ISR capabilities against peer/near-peer threats in highly contested environments, the US Air Force continues to fund efforts to maximise the Block 40's value to the Department of Defense until its planned divestiture in FY2027. Funding supports airspace, interoperability and communication updates, operational flight programme releases, airframe and software upgrades, and sensor enhancements. According to US Air Force budget documentation: "By FY2027, space-based capabilities and concepts of operation are planned to be in place to meet Combatant Commanders' needs in accordance with the National Defense Strategy."

Below: **An MQ-9 Reaper assigned to the 432nd Wing takes off from Creech Air Force Base, Nevada.** USAF/TSgt Emerson Nuñez

Notable Global Hawk events

In March 2023, the 7th RS based at Naval Air Station Sigonella, a geographically separated unit under the 319th Reconnaissance Wing, evaluated its ability to operate under the agile combat employment (ACE) concept of operations for the first time. The squadron deployed personnel, maintenance equipment and an RQ-4 aircraft to Larissa Air Base, Greece, and partnered with the Hellenic Air Force to operate from the base.

CURRENT COMBAT-CODED RQ-4 SQUADRONS

Squadron	Wing	Base	Major Command
4th RS	319th RW	Andersen Air Force Base, Guam	ACC
7th RS	319th RW	Naval Air Station Sigonella, Sicily	ACC
348th RS	319th RW	Grand Forks Air Force Base, North Dakota	ACC

Above: **Guardsmen assigned to the 174th Attack Wing based at Hancock Field Air National Guard Base, New York, place wheel chocks to stabilize an MQ-9 Reaper on the flightline following its arrival to Niagara Falls Air Reserve Station, New York.** USAF/SrA Kylar Vermeulen

Left: **Airmen assigned to the 7th Reconnaissance Squadron prepare to launch an RQ-4 Global Hawk at Naval Air Station Sigonella, Italy.** USAF/SSgt Ramon Adelan

On June 9, 2023, the 452nd Flight Test Squadron based at Edwards AFB held a sunset event for the RQ-4 Global Hawk flight test programme at the Californian super base. The event marked the completion of the squadron's test campaign for the aircraft.

An RQ-4B Global Hawk arrived at RAF Fairford, England, during the late evening on August 22, 2024, the first of the type to land in the UK. It had been on a mission to the Baltic region launched from Sigonella. The aircraft launched from Fairford late in the evening on August 24 and recovered to Sigonella. The night-time arrival and departure were intended to minimise the impact on civilian air traffic during its descent and climb from/to its operating altitude above 50,000ft.

The temporary deployment to Fairford helped to establish it as an alternative RQ-4B operating location within the European theatre and supported United States Air Forces in Europe – Air Forces Africa's implementation of the US Air Force's ACE concept of operations, which involves aircraft operating from alternate airfields to enhance survivability.

The RQ-4B involved was assigned to the 7th RS, a geographically separated unit of the 319th Reconnaissance Wing based at Grand Forks AFB, North Dakota, based at Naval Air Station Sigonella.

CURRENT COMBAT-CODED MQ-9 SQUADRONS

Squadron	Wing	Base	Major Command
11th Attack Squadron (ATKS)	432nd Wing, 432nd OG	Creech AFB, Nevada	ACC
15th ATKS	432nd Wing, 732nd OG	Creech AFB, Nevada	Nevada Air National Guard (ANG), Air Force Reserve Command (AFRC)
17th ATKS	432nd Wing, 732nd OG	Creech AFB, Nevada	Nevada ANG, AFRC
20th ATKS	432nd Wing, 25th Attack Group (ATKG)	Whiteman AFB, Missouri	ACC
22nd ATKS	432nd Wing, 732nd OG	Creech AFB, Nevada	Nevada ANG, AFRC
50th ATKS	432nd Wing, 25th ATKG	Shaw AFB, South Carolina	ACC
78th ATKS	432nd Wing, 726th OG	Nellis AFB, Nevada	AFRC TFI
89th ATKS	432nd Wing, 25th ATKG	Ellsworth AFB, South Dakota	ACC
91st ATKS	432nd Wing, 726th OG	Nellis AFB, Nevada	AFRC TFI
103rd ATKS	111th ATKW GCS	Horsham AGS, Pennsylvania	Pennsylvania ANG
105th ATKS	118th Wing GCS	Nashville Berry Field ANGB, Tennessee	Tennessee ANG
111th ATKS	147th ATKW MQ-9 and GCS	Ellington Field, Texas	Texas ANG
124th ATKS	132nd Wing GCS	Des Moines Airport, Iowa	Iowa ANG
136th ATKS	107th ATKW GCS	Niagara Falls ARS (MCE) and Wheeler AAF (LRE), New York	New York ANG
138th ATKS	174th ATKW MQ-9 and GCS	Hancock Field ANGB, New York	New York ANG
162nd ATKS	178th Wing GCS	Springfield-Beckley Airport, Ohio	Ohio ANG
172nd ATKS	110th ATKW GCS	Battle Creek ANGB, Michigan	Michigan ANG
178th ATKS	119th Wing MQ-9 and GCS	Fargo-Hector Airport, North Dakota	North Dakota ANG
184th ATKS	188th Wing GCS	Ebbing ANGB, Arkansas	Arkansas ANG
196th ATKS	163rd ATKW MQ-9 and GCS	March ARB, California	California ANG
214th ATKS	162nd Wing 214th ATKG MQ-9 and GCS	Davis Monthan AFB (MCE) and Libby AAF (LRE), Arizona	Arizona ANG
482nd ATKS	432nd Wing, 25th ATKG	Shaw AFB, South Carolina	ACC
489th ATKS	432nd Wing, 432nd OG	Creech AFB, Nevada	ACC
867th ATKS	432nd Wing, 732nd OG	Creech AFB, Nevada	Nevada ANG, AFRC
3rd Special Operations Squadron (SOS)	27th Special Operations Wing (SOW)	Cannon AFB, New Mexico	Air Force Special Operations Command (AFSOC)
12th SOS	27th SOW	Cannon AFB, New Mexico	AFSOC
33rd SOS	27th SOW	Cannon AFB, New Mexico	AFSOC
65th SOS	1st SOW	Hurlburt Field, Florida	AFSOC

Desert Base, Desert Ops

The 432nd Wing is the host unit at Creech AFB, located in the middle of the Mojave Desert in Nevada. Attack squadrons assigned to the wing's 432nd OG employs MQ-9 uncrewed aircraft in round-the-clock combat air patrols in support of combatant commander requirements and deploys what are referred to as combat support forces worldwide. The MQ-9's primary mission is strike, but is also widely utilised to gather real-time data to combatant commanders and intelligence specialists.

MQ-9 Reaper

According to official US Air Force documentation, the basic MQ-9 Reaper system "…consists of the aircraft, sensors, ground control station (GCS), communications equipment, weapon kits, and support and training equipment. The system is designed to be modular and open-ended. Mission-specific equipment

is employed in a plug-and-play mission kit concept allowing specific aircraft and GCS configurations to be tailored to fit mission needs".

Primarily, a strike asset used to employ precision-guided munitions and Hellfire missiles against various types of targets, its much-utilised tactical ISR capability using its multi-spectral camera, is the reason for including the MQ-9 in this review of US Air Force ISR systems.

Air Combat Command operates dozens of MQ-9s based at multiple locations around the United States and those forward deployed to locations around the world. The largest MQ-9 main operating base is Creech AFB, the

Above: **Operating from Naval Air Station Sigonella, Italy, the 7th Reconnaissance Squadron performs maintenance and launch and recovery operations to supply airborne Global Hawks to pilots at Beale Air force Base, California.** USAF/ SSgt Ramon Adelan

Left: **An MQ-9 Reaper flying to the range during Exercise Northern Strike near Alpena, Michigan.** USAF/ MSgt Scott Thompson

type's original home and that of the 432nd Wing, the only unit equipped with Block 1 and the upgraded Block 5 Reaper aircraft.

The US Air Force has established the MQ-9 Multi-Domain Operation (M2DO) aircraft configuration which consists of multiple projects intended to keep the platform viable in the wide-spectrum of armed conflict. The configuration includes anti-jam GPS, enhanced power, Link-16, an open mission system, and enhanced data processing. The number of M2DO aircraft, and final capabilities within this configuration has yet to be decided.

A small number of US Air Force MQ-9 Reaper aircraft carry a system called Gorgon Stare which captures wide-area motion imagery (WAMI) and distributes multiple live imagery streams via integrated line-of-sight and beyond line-of-sight datalinks to command authorities and ground units. According to the system's manufacturer, the Sierra Nevada Corporation, all WAMI captured throughout the full field-of-view of the multiple cameras housed in the system pods is stored in an accessible archive to support post-mission analysis.

Above: **An MQ-9 Reaper readied for flight during Exercise Northern Strike 2025 at the Alpena, Michigan Combat Regional Training Center in August 2025.** USANG/SMSgt Michael Knodle

Left: **An RQ-4B Global Hawk assigned to the 319th Reconnaissance Wing under tow at RAF Fairford during the type's maiden deployment to England in support of allied and US forces around the European Command area of responsibility.** USAF/TSgt Jessica Avallone

The Gorgon Stare system can fulfil ISR requirements on land, at sea, and in the air.

An MQ-9 aircrew comprises a pilot and a sensor operator. From take-off to landing, the aircraft is controlled by a pilot sat at a console inside a ground control station. During the take-off run, the pilot uses a forward-looking nose-mounted camera for visual reference to make sure the aircraft is tracking straight down the runway. The pilot can choose to use either a daytime electro-optical or night-time infrared camera, or the MTS (Multi-spectral Targeting System) sensor mounted under the forward fuselage.

Aircrews assigned to the 432nd fly either the LRE or the MCE, an arrangement known as split operation. Each element is linked to the aircraft via satellite.

Explaining the primary reason for splitting operations between LRE and MCE elements, Maj Troy (surname withheld for security reasons) said: "When you're flying via satellite here in the States, you have to encrypt the satellite signal. That way hostile forces cannot hack into the signal and take command of the air vehicle. Encryption causes a delay in your input when you're flying via satellite. For example, if I command the aircraft to make a right turn via satellite, it suffers from a one second delay to respond to the command. That's not conducive for a take-off or a landing

Above: **Airmen push an MQ-9 Reaper into a hangar during Exercise Northern Strike at Alpena, Michigan.** USAF/MSgt Scott Thompson

Below: **An MTS camera screen grab showing munitions exploding on a range during Exercise Northern Strike near Alpena, Michigan.** USAF/MSgt Scott Thompson

where your control inputs need an immediate response. To mitigate that, personnel deploy to forward operating locations where they use a different architecture for aircraft take-off and landing. A ground data terminal beams the input direct to the aircraft via line of sight with an instantaneous response. That allows the pilot to take-off and land more smoothly.

"A ground data terminal is limited by range. Once range is exceeded, you can no longer control the air vehicle via line of sight. So, we divvy up the operations by using a concept known as remote split ops. Personnel deployed to a forward operating location launch the aircraft and fly it to

a safe location. And aircrews operating from ground control stations at Creech will turn on the satellite link, grab the aircraft, and fly their mission. Once the air vehicle is at its return-to-base fuel state, the MCE fly it back to a safe area from where the deployed LRE turn on the ground data terminal, grab the aircraft and land it."

An LRE pilot starts their launch process with an aircraft parked on the flight line. The pilot starts the engine, taxies out, ensures the systems, including the line-of-sight connection, are functioning correctly and conducts the take-off. Designated areas are used for the hand over. Troy explained how the pilot flies the MQ-9 to a safe

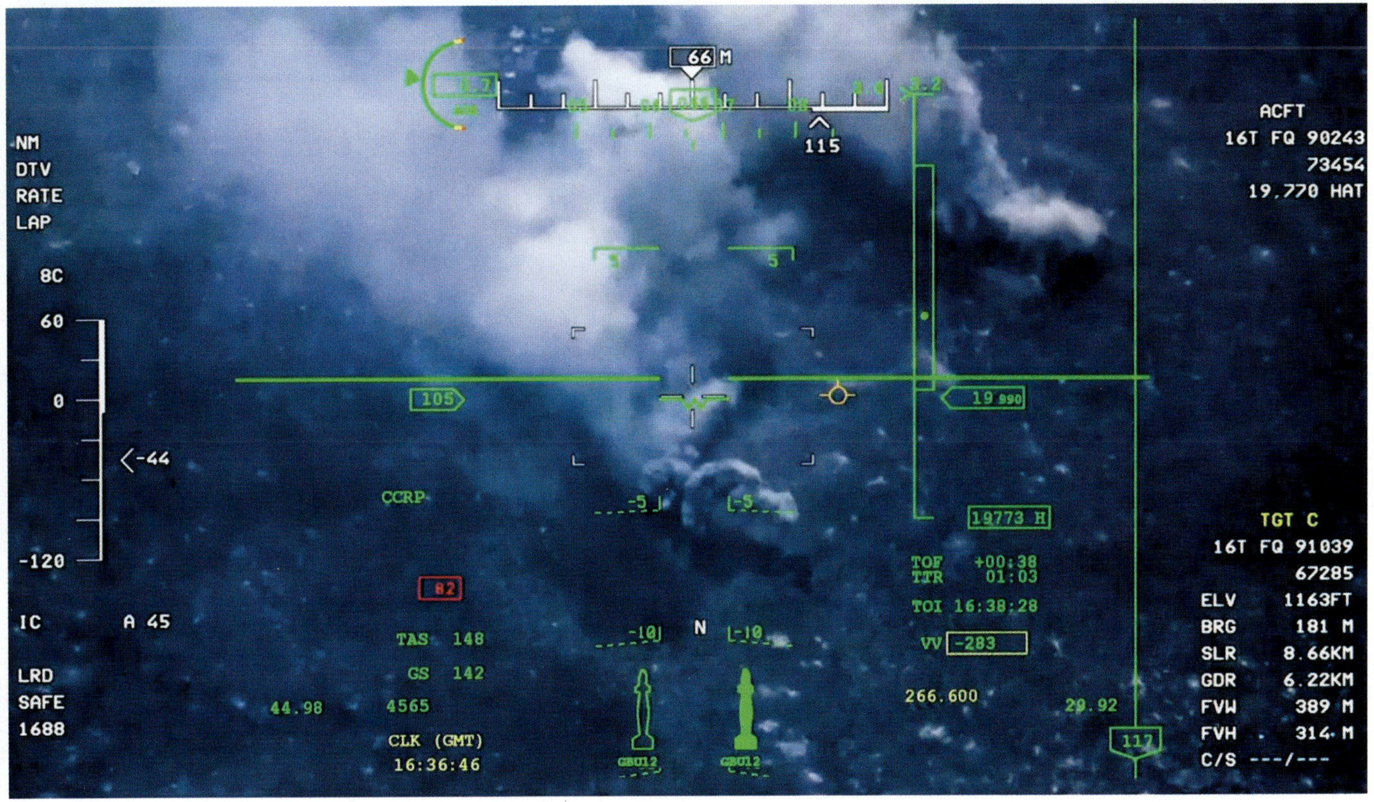

Above: **Airmen pose for a group photo in front of an RQ-4B Global Hawk assigned to the 319th Reconnaissance Wing at RAF Fairford on August 24, 2024, during the first RQ-4B deployment to England.** USAF/TSgt Jessica Avallone

Right: **An MQ-9 Reaper taxies along the flightline at Creech Air Force Base, Nevada.** USAF/Senior Airman Victoria Nuzzi

altitude and location, and with a simple mouse click command places the air vehicle in a pre-planned orbit. "We then advise the MCE crew we're going to shut off the aircraft's LRE connection, which always has precedence. If two elements are both trying to grab the aircraft, one via satellite and one via the ground data terminal, the line-of-sight connection always trumps the satellite connection. The LRE pilot must turn off the connection before the MCE can grab the aircraft which is why the LRE pilot tells the MCE of the disconnection. At the time, the MCE has their satellite link ready to grab the aircraft. Similarly at the end of the mission, the MCE flies the air vehicle to a safe area of airspace and advises the LRE of the air vehicle entering its pre-planned orbit. The MCE severs the connection, and the LRE grabs control of the air vehicle using the ground data terminal for recovery to the base."